CONCILIUM

D1607940

CONCILIUM 2007/3

AIDS

Edited by
Regina Ammicht-Quinn
Hille Hacker

SCM Press · London

Published by SCM Press, 13–17 Long Lane, London EC1A 9PN

ISBN 978 0 334 03094 2

Printed and bound in Great Britain by
William Clowes Ltd, Beccles, Suffolk

Concilium published February, April, June, October
December

Contents

Message Concerning Jon Sobrino's Christology

For us, the directors of *Concilium*, and for many people throughout the world, Jon Sobrino reflects on the Christian message of salvation in a way that is relevant for our journeys of faith. We wholeheartedly admire and thank our colleague and friend, and we praise God that in 1989 he was not killed like his fellow Jesuits and two women serving in his house in San Salvador.

All theological discourse falls short of the mystery of God's love in and through Jesus Christ. That is why every theologian is in the process of learning the fullness of truth. Jon Sobrino has an exemplary theological attitude of teaching and of learning from others, so as to understand the liberating truth of Jesus Christ, witnessed by the community of the Church.

The recent *Notification* by the Congregation of the Doctrine of the Faith (26 Nov. 2006, made public in March 2007) disregards the theological developments of the last fifty years and uses a deductive argumentation that is unable to do justice to Jon Sobrino's contextual and hermeneutical approach and his scholarly engagement with exegetical and theological developments.

We are convinced that Sobrino's Christology is faithful to the gospel, and that it fosters theological growth in the Church. The *Notification* says that his writings contain 'notable discrepancies with the faith of the Church'. It may be asked who the theologians are whose views are taken as the basis for the *Notification*, and what kind of hermeneutics they wish to impose. The Sobrino case has implications for how the teaching authority of the Church deals with theologians, as much as for how theologians relate to the faith of the poor of the world. We are committed to service within our Church, to necessary theological debates, and to solidarity with all human beings who strive for justice, peace, and the integrity of creation.

We sincerely thank Jon Sobrino for his challenging contributions, and as directors of the journal *Concilium* we will continue our dialogue with all who seek truth and justice.

DIRECTORS OF *CONCILIUM, International Journal of Theology*

Foreword

DR PETER PIOT, DIRECTOR OF UNAIDS

As the world unites in efforts to scale up action against AIDS it is vital we further explore the role and potential of Churches in playing their part.

Churches are established and important partners in responding to AIDS and in caring for people living with HIV; communities of faith have often provided refuge for people from some of the stigma and discrimination in society. At the same time, unfortunately, faith communities can also be places that reinforce stigma; effective action can be paralyzed by an unwillingness to address the issues men and women are facing in their daily lives.

UNAIDS encourages churches, theologians, and communities of faith to continue to grapple with the difficult issues presented by AIDS – many of which are expressed by the authors in this issue of *Concilium*. I am pleased to provide these introductory comments and congratulate all contributors for an interesting and challenging set of reflections on AIDS.

While it would be impossible for all stakeholders to agree on every issue connected to AIDS, the challenge ahead of us is to strive together to identify areas of synergy and to move forward together with concrete actions to bring clear, evidence-informed HIV prevention messages and quality treatment and care programmes to people in need.

In my younger days as a doctor in Africa in the early days of AIDS I realized that this disease would be of such magnitude that it was going to take a response of global proportions to make a real difference.

My worst fear today is that as a global community our response will fall short of what is still needed and history will turn to our generation and ask us why we did not do enough when we knew what was needed to stop this pandemic. But although AIDS can divide it can also unite people from diverse backgrounds in phenomenal ways. One of my biggest hopes is that AIDS gives us an opportunity to overcome our differences, whether they are religious, political, or geographical, and to work together on a response that will turn the tide of this pandemic.

Hope for a better future is what continues to drive us in our work against

AIDS. The AIDS epidemic is not only about revealing injustice but also about overcoming injustice. With this in mind there are a number of key challenges for Churches working on AIDS.

First is the challenge of engaging young people. Wherever HIV has been pushed back, it was young people who have been at the forefront of this change. Churches need to adapt their teachings to the realities of young people and of women, and, in the case of AIDS, it is vital to deal openly with questions regarding sexuality. Churches may preach moral virtues such as abstinence and monogamy, but they also need to give support to young people for achieving simpler goals, such as postponing sexual activity until they are older, understanding risk, and knowing where to get advice and condoms to protect themselves against infection.

A further challenge is that posed by stigma. HIV-related stigma is a very heavy burden that limits the effectiveness of AIDS programmes. We need Churches to further unite and act against stigma and discrimination in order to support our AIDS responses.

Finally, the great challenge posed to communities in accessing treatment. Churches and church leaders can strengthen their advocacy in ensuring that treatment reaches the poorest and neediest. Health care facilities run by church groups need to be included in national plans to scale up access to treatment and care services.

Leadership, from the grassroots within Churches and from church hierarchies themselves, is an important lever for the global fight against AIDS.

Despite the many achievements of the global AIDS movement, we are still far from our goal to reverse this epidemic by 2015. The work of Churches is a vital part of strengthening the fight against AIDS, until we achieve universal access to essential services and have turned the tide for good against this epidemic.

Editorial

Why publish an issue of *Concilium* on HIV/AIDS, when so much has already been written on the epidemic? In his Foreword Peter Piot has expressed the answer much more effectively than we could ever manage: because the Churches' efforts are needed in the struggle against AIDS. We have produced this issue because there has been so much misunderstanding (which includes theological misunderstanding) that has to be examined in the area under discussion; because *Concilium* has never devoted a single number to an explicit study of HIV/AIDS; and last but not least because Catholic theology and its environs feature so much important consideration of the subject that we feel must surely interest our readers.

Language is necessarily the medium proper to a journal. In this case, we have tried to be somewhat more experimental than in the past. We have also tried to find a theologically appropriate way of talking about an illness that is not easy to tackle in linguistic terms. We have tried to avoid stuffing as much information as possible into the least possible space. That is not our task and, if you want it, you can soon find it in other media. Instead we have tried not only to show the faces behind the figures and facts but to attempt the task proper to our calling: which is to do our best to provide analyses from a theological viewpoint and to develop proposals for theological practice in this respect. Since both editors offer their own contributions at the end of this issue, we shall confine ourselves here to thanking all those who have taken part in this experiment.

We are most grateful to Ignace Berten, Virgilio Elizondo, Mary Hunt, Harry McSorley, Eloi Messi Metogo and – especially – Marcella Althaus-Reid for help with the preparation of this issue. We wish to thank the directors of *Concilium* for their comments and assistance, the secretariat in Nijmegen, particularly Christine van Wijnbergen and Erik Borgman, the translators, and all those responsible at the various publishing houses concerned.

I. AIDS in Different Regions

Integrating Long-term HIV Patients in Brazil

LISETTE AND PETER EICHER

'I have loved so much! I have suffered so much!' (Oswald de Andrade)

Stars stand out against a dark sky

For three hundred years – until 1888 – the Portuguese abused Africans as slaves in Brazil. Some of their descendants still live together with various groups excluded from modern industrial society in the mean hovels of the shanty-towns or *favelas*, in the half-day rented bunks of the narrow *cortiços* (slum tenements), in the hazardous *mocós* (stygian recesses below bridges), and simply on the streets. All these living-spaces are even more miserable than the *senzalas*, as the old plantation slave quarters were known. Twenty per cent of the inhabitants of the major cities of Brazil live in *lixo*, in the garbage of a continually outgrowing world, yet also amidst the *luxo*, the superfluity of the consumer society from which their fellow–citizens profit. For twenty-one years the military dictatorship tried to enthuse the poor masses of Brazil for the ideology of progress and used repression to hide poverty and suffering. When democracy finally supervened in 1985 and a new social outlook seemed on the cards, a sinister visitant appeared in the dark lower depths of society in the form of death-dealing AIDS. A fatal AIDS pandemic joined forces with extreme privation among the involuntary dregs of the community.

Nevertheless, a spark of hope was struck in the all but impenetrable darkness of social destitution and implacable infection. From 1987 onwards, at the invitation of Cardinal Evaristo Arns, we[1] were in São Paulo to care for

13

those suffering from AIDS in the underworld of a population of, then, sixteen million.[2] Since there were neither beds nor premises in which to look after people in the totally impoverished areas of the city, the headquarters of the Franciscan missions and the aid organization Misereor (which is supported by the hierarchy in Germany) made it possible to buy a large tract of land in the north east of the city. This *terra da promessa,* or 'promised land', became the basis of what in the meantime has grown into the largest aid organization for impoverished mothers, children, and marginalized people living with and dying from HIV in Latin America. The internationally supported 'Star of Hope' association[3] has enabled more than eighty people working in thirty houses to provide medical care using the most up-to-date means for those affected, and has allowed them to go to good schools and to become socially integrated.

To ensure that the human experience of those who have died from AIDS is not permanently suppressed, communicators are needed to relate details of their lives and deaths. Dead AIDS victims are not forgotten in Brazil, a country of imaginative literature. These narratives have helped to ensure that HIV-positive people in Brazil are now socially integrated to a degree met with in very few other countries in the world: in health policy, in the world of work, in media awareness, in religious affairs, and in terms of social solidarity. In order to contribute these sparks of hope from Brazil to the efforts to illuminate the darkness of the worldwide epidemic, the following is offered as an account of the four phases of the relevant process in Brazil, together with the stories of certain individuals whose experiences and vision have been entrusted to us as an inspiration for the future.

I. Panic (1985–1990)

Rosilene was a confirmed solitary. Her mother abandoned her when she was four. She was educated by nuns and at sixteen took to the urban desert of São Paulo. When a sweet-talking white boy named Carlos introduced her to love-making, the young mulatto girl broke all bounds. They slept in still open graves in a cemetery, and supped on the smog of the city streets; her engagement present was pregnancy. Carlos worked in a motel. Together with his love he gave her the deadly virus. Lesions of the central nervous system and Kaposi's sarcoma made him a shadow of his former self. But love and death have always been close companions (as Nietzsche remarked). Rosilene swore that she would kill her lover if her child was HIV-positive at birth.

'We found her at an advanced stage of pregnancy on the street. We had no bed, house, or refuge. The house belonging to an aid organization was torched because it was rumoured that AIDS patients were looked after there.

'An affecting rehearsal of the Christmas story persuaded a Legion of Mary group to make their house available to us for a time for the care of expelled AIDS patients. It was there that Rosilene gave her son the "light of the world", as they say in Brazil. The Bishop of Santana baptized the new-born child Raphael, which means "God cures". But Raphael became severely ill, for he had been infected at birth – at that time it was thought that he had been infected in his mother's womb. In desperation Rosilene locked her Carlos indoors, for he no longer recognized anyone and had fallen in the bath – he died from the results of the fall. Rosilene wandered about with her child for a few days. Then Raphael died too. Rosilene smiled again when she walked along the beach gathering shell-fish. Then she reverted to her former solitary way of life.'

The United States and South America were the first to be affected. In 1981 gay men from San Francisco exhibiting terrifying symptoms were dying from an unknown new disease. Even before the virus was identified in 1983, young men were presenting with symptoms that included those of Kaposi's sarcoma (cancerous indurations of the skin), oesophageal candidiasis (a kind of fungus), reactivated toxoplasma gondii (and primary central nervous system lymphomas, including brain lesions), tuberculosis, and skeletal emaciation. Something hitherto inconceivable was happening: handing on life was changing into handing on death. Blood and sex, taboo areas and symbols of life, became mortally dangerous.

The reaction was panic. And panic resulted in criminal acts against sufferers. No medical explanation of the symptoms was forthcoming. This disaster just did not fit the picture of any previous epidemic, such as plague, cholera, or even syphilis. There was no way of stopping the outbreak of the disease, and no possibility of alleviating the bizarre signs of Kaposi's sarcoma, which was more pronounced in Brazil than in the USA or in Europe. Brazil of all countries was where the virus spread most rapidly and where those affected were most likely to die very soon. Many families cast off their infected children or locked them in. Gangs of *exterminadores* (exterminators) murdered AIDS patients on the streets of the poor quarters quite openly. No one reported the killers.

During the ten years of panic reaction, the modern confidence about our ability to control life was shattered. No one had expected scientific medicine to be totally powerless in the face of a pandemic of this kind. In addition, given the economic crisis, inflation, and the unjust distribution of assets and profits, signs of any hope in the power of political action to change things in those respects were only just beginning to reappear in Brazil. But at that time neither medicine nor politics nor religion could offer any suggestions about dealing with, or even merely alleviating, this dramatically spreading epidemic.[4]

Liberation theology faded from the scene in this regard. It fell into the trap, as it were, of its own presumptions. Expectation of the kingdom of God was the basis of its demand for the establishment of social justice. But liberation theologians saw things in terms of the philosophy of history and socio-political theory; they were less inclined to categorize and examine phenomena from the viewpoint of different cultures and almost never paid attention to natural categories. But in this case nature was operating quite cruelly and was indifferent to all considerations of human dignity and justice. It is not so surprising that at that time cardinals, bishops, and con-servative theologians should have attributed the responsibility for AIDS to those suffering from the disease and vilified them in their last agony as queers, liberal scum, and irresponsible degenerates. The dogmatic interpre-tation of the theodicy problem insisted that the ultimate responsibility for the absurdity of suffering had to be ascribed to human beings and to its victims. What was really astonishing, however, was the inability of liberation theologians to conceptualize or express the new situation, apart from a few recommendations that were merely somewhat more liberal than others from the angle of moral theology. Liberation theology had nothing to say because it was stuck with the paradigm of historical change. This meant that its adherents could see illness only as a social event and not as something that happened to human beings. There was no option for the people who were dying of AIDS. In the Church, too, they would just have to keep out of the way, and stay hidden while they died – which was especially true as far as HIV-positive priests were concerned.

II. Caring for the dying (up to 1997)

'João wasn't deaf but he was almost completely dumb. The virus had made him skeletal. He always kept his head down in front of others and it was all but impossible to look him in the eyes. He would nod vigorously if questioned, so we discovered that he would like to keep chickens. Since we still had no land, we bought him some quails which he was very keen on and cared for devotedly. After many questions, we also found out something confirmed later by medical tests: as a small boy João had been severely abused and became dumb as a result. On one occasion after a long stay we were already in the car ready to take us to the airport for the flight back home when the news reached us that João was dying in the hospital for infectious diseases, and wanted to tell us something. We were surprised that he had been able to communicate so precise a message. We just had time to drive by and call in at the hospital. A beaming João was sitting up on the bed in a room on his own. He talked to us clearly, without inhibition, and quite endearingly. The fear that had silenced him had disappeared. He embraced us as if he were our brother. We left, and three days later we learned that he was dead.

'In this period, in the Star of Hope facilities in São Paulo alone, we were able to help, care for and find room for three thousand people suffering from full-blown AIDS'.[5]

Even in the face of disasters, Brazilians are imaginative. In the early 1990s, creative rhetoric, celebration, and an ability to set up groups gradually released the population from their trauma. Now AIDS became the main topic of imaginative discourse and media discussion, and the focus of charitable efforts and public interest. The initial excommunication from society and from the community of the morally unassailable turned into an ethically based concern – a kind of charitable love of your enemy that led the more courageous helpers to try to provide those suffering from the deadly virus with a place and space in which to die. Since the number of those infected increased dramatically, and babies, mothers, children, and older people of both sexes now carried the virus, the HIV-positives who had been declared responsible became the sacrificial victims of the epidemic. Victims deserve charitable aid. Now the theme of care for those who mourn and are dying was imported from the USA and literarily translated into 'Brazilian'. Hundreds of groups were formed which in various ways all over the country made AIDS the target of preventative measures and the occasion for devising new forms of caring for the needy and suffering.

Even at that stage, three ways of dealing with the crisis were already characteristic of the now well-known uniquely Brazilian approach to the disease: philanthropic recourse to justice, the practical expression of solidarity with the victims, and religious acceptance of die absurdity of suffering.

Before all other countries, Brazil enshrined in the constitution the human right to full realization of the dignity of all HIV-positive people and to a comprehensive entitlement to full care, and in thousands of individual enactments at all levels in cities and towns, the various States, and the Federal State itself. All discriminative demonstrations, actions, and injunctions against HIV-sufferers in the media, schools, firms, and public bodies were expressly prohibited. This included all involuntary HIV tests. All hospitals, all private doctors, and dentists had to treat HIV-positives. Dismissals or disadvantages on account of HIV – a policy still applied as a matter of course to those seeking to enter Roman Catholic religious Orders and the priesthood – were forbidden on pain of severe penalties. 'No one', we read, for instance, in clause 14 of the 1994 Paraiba Health Care Act, 'shall have the right to limit an individual's freedom or entitlement on the sole ground that the person in question is an HIV carrier, and this shall be the case irrespective of that person's race, gender, nationality, religion, ideology, or sexual orientation.' The philanthropic rhetoric of Brazilian legislation in this respect must be unique throughout the world. Essentially, however, it protects the human rights of those who are HIV-positive and therefore legally defends a nuanced ethics. There is still a considerable gulf between this viewpoint and the moral theology of the Roman Catholic Church. The legislation of some individual States in Brazil requires the proprietors of motels to make at least four in-date condoms available to a guest free of charge (João Pessoa, Law 7.629, of 15 July 1994, clause 10), and requires schools to teach and discuss drug use and sexually transmissible diseases with pupils from the fifth primary class at least once a month (*id.*, Law 7.353 of 17 August 1993, clause 10).

The lack of national health and insurance forces the poor and the distressed masses to look after themselves. Nevertheless, in the midst of all calamities caused by need, a certain ethos of the Brazilian poor has fostered an impressively warm physical expression[6] of solidarity and impassioned sharing. The typically Brazilian form of physicality, derived from African and indigenous origins, is world-famous, but its manifestations, apart from the samba, football, the dance-fight *capoeira*, and carnival are scarcely known outside Brazil. In reality, however, physical solidarity is practised extensively in neighbourly assistance, the tangible organization of solutions to a chaotic existence, and robust forms of defence against exploitation. During the AIDS catastrophe the culture of the poor has produced a new and richly inventive solidarity of endangered bodies. The physical, indeed sensual, creativity that is part of the common ethos of the Brazilian poor appears in the liturgy and social work of quite conservative parishes; in the Brazilian variants of Voodoo known as Candomblé, Umbanda, and Macumba; in the mass celebrations of the Pentecostal Churches; in the soccer fan-clubs organized by various communities; and in hundreds of groups and occasions by and for HIV sufferers. In the country's vast urban environments, condoms are treated more as toys or as objects of derision rather than actually used to prevent disease, so that dicing with death can also be an aspect of this vigorous passion for a physical and sensual existence.

Eighty-five per cent of the total population of Brazil live in towns and cities, and 20 per cent in cities with more than one million inhabitants. In sociological terms they are mainly incomers from the countryside, ethnologically uprooted people, who cling to the remnants of archaic traditions. As far as religion is concerned, Brazilians affected by mass impoverishment (at least 25 per cent of the population) live with their own inimitable concepts of the divine. Their life and death, as they say, 'happen with God' – with angels, spirits, and demons. Invoking their relationship with those pagan divinities of African origin known as *Orixás*, many mortally infected people entrust themselves to angels for support or to spirits for protection. No discussion of AIDS takes place without a reference to *graças à Deus* – and at all events not without a guilt-ridden fear of hell.

The vast increase in fundamentalist and charismatic movements indicates the need of excessively burdened individuals to escape their isolation by joining crisis cults. Their embodiment of solidarity is evident in rhythmical singing. Rhythm is a symbolic form of bursting through the boundaries of the 'here and now'. Unlike the Catholic Church in this respect, the Pentecostal Churches entertained the belief that it was possible to cure AIDS by prayer and the laying on of hands. In the 1990s, on the other hand, the Catholic and Lutheran Churches, but also the Adventists and the Afro-Brazilian Candomblé, Macumba, and Umbanda cults concentrated emphatically on realistic social aid in the context of AIDS in spite of the growing interest in their rites. But, like the new Pentecostal Church of the *Assembleia de Deus*, the evangelical and fundamentalist Churches, and the Mormons and Baptists, the Catholic hierarchy never scrapped its assertion that the best protection from AIDS was abstinence before and outside marriage. 'The sexual bond of chastity is the only safe and the only virtuous means to put an end to AIDS, this tragic affliction' (Pope John Paul II, 6.2.1993). Not merely the Catholic Church but all Churches had to combat prejudice and discrimination against HIV-positives in their own ranks, because many preachers continued to explain AIDS as the embodiment of sin, as God's punishment, and as a prediction of everlasting damnation. Most Churches also continued to reject, though to varying degrees, homosexuality as a way of life and as one among other forms of love. An embarrassing phenomenon in regard to the moral approach to AIDS in Brazil was provided by the publications of Padre Valeriano Paitoni (of the Missionaries of the

Consolata). He was a priest with a considerable degree of social commitment, and active in the field of AIDS. He wrote articles for the international press citing the relatively high numbers of priests suffering from HIV. Another aspect of Brazilian realism was that the infected priests were not allowed to reveal that they were sick, and when they came to die were separated from parishes and communities in a strictly out of bounds hospice called 'Calvaria'. Furthermore, at that time no HIV-positive priests and Religious were officially allowed to take an active part in AIDS pastoral work.

III. Checking the deathly sickness (1996–1997)

'Eloisa is a poet. She makes her passionate verses rhyme neatly, and every day discovers the childhood she never experienced. She lost her mother when she was four. Her father put her in an orphanage and disappeared for ever. We found Eloisa on the street; she was pregnant, HIV-positive and sick. All she cared about was the future of her child, whom she would never be able to care for. Eloisa saw how all the others were dying from the virus and thought she didn't have a chance.

'Things turned out quite differently. As still often happens with black mothers, she was over the moon when she found out that her baby was born blond and had white skin. The community would accept him as a full human being. Therefore she gave him up for adoption, so that her boy would be the legally certified son of solidly-established upper middle-class parents. All she wanted to do now was to die in peace.

'She lived.

'The new drugs arrived, seemingly out of the blue. Her immunity was very soon re-established on the basis of the new triple combination drug regimen. That was in 1997. Now Eloisa is living in fine shape – though without her child – in her own little stone house, made available to her by the Star of Hope association. Almost every day she writes a poem for her son, who is quite *au fait* with the situation. She wants him to know that she voluntarily surrendered him for adoption because she loved him. Eloisa has founded her own Star of Hope organization. In her one-room home she occasionally puts up AIDS-sufferers, HIV-positives, and people living on the edge.'

In 1996 and 1997 a whole series of drugs inhibiting protease and reverse transcriptase passed the pharmaceutical tests for release. In combination, these anti-retroviral drugs have totally changed the nature of the epidemic, and produced an unexpectedly impressive diminution of the number of patients and of deaths. In particular, the drive to prevent infection at birth has been definitively successful. Since 1997, not one baby born to an HIV-positive mother has been infected in Star of Hope enterprises. The aid given with high-risk births and the threefold combination therapy prevent the infection that occurred formerly at birth or through the mother's milk. All HIV-positives and AIDS-sufferers and all those living or working with them experienced this as something like a transition from night to day. Even though the ultimately terminal immune deficiency cannot be cured by the present generation of drugs developed to combat the disease, the considerable extension of life, the removal of some and in certain cases of all symptoms, and especially the possibility of conceiving and giving birth to disease-free children are immense boons. All those who lived with HIV-positive people before and after the drugs to fight it arrived cannot understand why every government in the world is not prepared to let all HIV-patients have the benefit of the medicines they need. The difference in the quality of life between those receiving and those without the drugs is like that between normal life and hell.

Brazil is one of the few countries in the world that is prepared to pay for comprehensive prevention in all areas of risk and, since the release of the combination-drug treatment, for the issue free of charge of all new medicines to all patients.[7] Brazil is also the country that has enshrined in the constitution this prevention and these drugs as a right and duty. Brazil has recognized that the socially preventative and medical treatment of AIDS is a matter of basic human entitlement, of entitlement to life.[8]

The epidemic has become a social and ethical challenge for aid organizations, for state social welfare, and for the Churches.[9] Now more is needed than any kind of hospice movement that seeks to ensure that those affected can die with dignity. Now it is necessary to make prevention compulsory, to offer patients the medically appropriate treatment, and to reintegrate them effectively in society. That is how Brazil came to choose its particular way of dealing with the problem. Whereas the epidemic continues to expand in Africa, Eastern Europe, Asia and China, in Brazil it is becoming a disease that is admittedly fatal in the long term, but one with a controlled course, and one that is often asymptomatic for very long periods. In the midst of the continuing scandal of impoverishment and marginalization of HIV carriers,[10] the new ethos of integration came into being in Brazil.[11] It is a sign of hope for other countries' treatment of those suffering from the HIV virus.

IV. Integration (since 1999)

'In all disasters it is the children's eyes, their questioning and laughter that reconfigure the world. She had had four abortions, said Maira, to make sure that she did not bring an HIV-positive child into the world. When she became pregnant again, she heard of the Star of Hope association and gained the courage to give birth. The eyes of her Alexandre, who has been attending an elementary school for four years now, have become the central challenge of her life. Maira works in our hydroponic facility and in the bakery (subsidized by Elton John), so she will soon be able to afford her own little house. The totally unexpected has happened. Every day now the same people who a few years ago did everything possible to distance themselves from AIDS buy the bread and lettuce produced by HIV-positive patients. Their confidence has been restored.'

Since 1999, in response to pressure from the World Bank and from UNAIDS, but also as a result of creative indigenous initiatives, Brazil has implemented an innovative and hitherto unknown form of health policy at the Federal State level, and at that of individual states and of many district administrations. The State seeks to ensure cooperation with non-governmental aid organizations, the Churches, and all concerned, in order to bring immune deficiency under control. Similarly, the Catholic Bishops' Conference has taken the unusual step of setting up a working group that operates not only within the Church, and ecumenically in the usual sense of the word, but together with all other religious bodies, aid organizations, and officials at all levels. This has resulted in a new form of discourse about suffering, the human right to care, and international responsibility in the realm of health policy. The basis is still the free distribution of all medicines for all those in need by the State, and therefore financed ultimately by taxpayers. Nevertheless, to ensure realistic use of this health-policy contribution by State and society, the necessary infrastructures for monitored administration of drugs and care must be available among the affected groups.

The current problem is now evident.

We are no longer faced with outsider groups as those who become infected but – increasingly – with women living below the poverty level and with marginalized young people. Experience has shown that only encouragement of independent development can make possible the infrastructures needed to live with the virus in a context of prevention and control. But how can women in the north east of Brazil overcome the *machismo* of men with an archaic religious attitude who infect them by refusing to use any kind of preventative measure? How can the poor who have been thrust down into an underworld life in the cities attend for regular care and treatment? How can the twenty-three million children in Brazil without any adequate education learn how to live appropriately and with self-respect?

Since the use of antiretroviral drugs has made it possible to control the virus, the impression has spread in rich countries and among well-off groups in the population that those who are appropriately treated medically will make it at least relatively possible to control the problem of the epidemic, without any pressing need simultaneously to solve the problem of the pandemic in the poor regions of the world and among the impoverished groups in their own cities. For a while, the window on the poor and suffering of the world had been opened up to some degree, because the rich too were afraid that the disaster would spread from those below to those above. Accordingly, we now know very much more about actual sexual behaviour throughout the world than we did before the AIDS catastrophe. We also know very much more about the fatal mechanisms of impoverishment. The question is how theology can help the Churches to acquire knowledge of the preventative methods that are necessary in order to ameliorate the disease situation when treating and caring for those who are terminally affected by AIDS. The Brazilian experience shows that effective help can be provided only if medicine, the State, the pharmaceutical industry, education and religion work together to achieve this. In the AIDS era, religion has ceased to be a separate sector of existence.

Translated by J. G. Cumming

Notes

1. Lisette Eicher, the wife of Peter Eicher, a nurse and the mother of five children, moved to São Paulo for a whole year; Peter Eicher, who teaches at Paderborn University, was with his wife sporadically and organized help in Germany and in Switzerland.
2. Twenty-two million in 2007.
3. Cf. www.sternderhoffnung.de.
4. See: *DossiêAIDS*, *Revista USP* (São Paulo University), No. 33, 1989.
5. According to the information given by Cardinal Arns at the time, and by those in charge of the Emilio Ribas Fever Hospital, no one—not even church communities—buried dead paupers in the city.
6. Cf. Stephan Kriesel, *Der Körper als Paradigma. Leibesdiskurse in Kultur, Volksreligiosität und Theologie Brasiliens*, Lucerne, 2001.

7. See: UNAIDS, *Report on the global AIDS epidemic* (2006), part 3; SchaaberJörg, *Keine Medikamente für die Armen. Hindernisse auf dem Weg zu einer gerechten Arzeneimittelversorgung am Beispiel AIDS*, Frankfurt am Main, 2005, pp. 117ff.

8. See also, however, on the extreme inequality in Brazil, André Campos, *Atlas da exclusão social no Brasil*, Vol.2, São Paulo, 2003.

9. On Latin America in the critical phase of 1997 see Ricardo M. Caldéron, *Religious-Based Initiatives*, Arlington, Aidscap, 1997.

10. For an impressive case study of five children dying of AIDS, see Ana Maria Baricca, *Histórias vividas por crianças com AIDS*, São Paulo, Universidade de São Paulo, Instituto de Psicologia, 1998.

11. Cf. Mary Garcia Castro, Lorena Bernadete da Silva, *Responses to Aids. Challenges in Brazil: Limits and Possibilities*, Brasilia, Unesco and Ministry of Health, 2005. On the significance of the 'Alivi' aid efforts provided by 'Star of Hope', see *op. cit.*, pp. 327–36; and *AIDS: what young people think about it*, Brasilia, Unesco Brazil, 2004.

HIV/AIDS and Black Communities in Britain – Reflections from a Practical Black British Liberation Theologian

ANTHONY G. REDDIE

Introduction

In this essay, I shall be addressing the social mores and theological frameworks that have influenced the reaction of Black, African Caribbean peoples in Britain to the growing incidences of HIV/AIDS within their communities. I am writing this piece as a Practical Black Liberation theologian, whose principle area of expertise is in Liberative models of Christian education and formation that are cognisant of Black cultures and histories. I am not, I hasten to add, a specialist and I have not undertaken specialist work in HIV/AIDS. Here I simply want to offer a brief snapshot of how and for what reasons many African Caribbean Christian communities have been unwilling either to confront or to offer any meaningful support and pastoral care to those suffering from HIV/AIDS from within their ranks.

This work will be approached by means of some participatory field work I undertook some years ago[1] and to which I returned in order to write this essay. This initial work has been supplemented by a more recent return to one of the groups with whom I worked a number of years ago in order to continue the quest of teasing out their theological reflections on the whole nature of suffering and illness in respect of the scourge of HIV/AIDS.

I. Defining the context and my own position – locating myself

As a contextual theologian I am always wary of the people who do not locate either themselves or their work within any particular social or cultural milieu when they begin to explicate their ideas. I shall not make that elemental mistake.

I am an African Caribbean male Christian. I was born in Bradford, in

West Yorkshire, in 1964. My parents arrived in Britain in the late 1950s from the Caribbean island of Jamaica as part of the mass migratory movement of predominantly Black people from the so-called 'New Commonwealth',[2] the movement of Black people from Africa and the Caribbean in the years following the end of the Second War. The 1945 post-war presence of Black people within inner cities in Britain and the churches to be found there is a phenomenon that has been described by a great many sociologists and historians.[3] It is often believed that the existence of Black people in Britain can be traced to this period in British history. This influx is perceived as commencing with the arrival of 492 Jamaicans at Tilbury dock on the 'Empire Windrush' on 22 June 1948. Yet Ian Duffield, quoting from *The Gentlemen's Magazine* of 1764 describes the large numbers of Black people, estimated at the time to be as high as 20,000, living in London at the turn of the eighteenth century.[4]

Peter Fryer describes the sense of alarm within London society in the later years of the reign of Elizabeth I at the apparently large numbers of Black people, which Fryer estimates to be around 10,000 living in the capital at that time.[5] Black people have lived in Britain far longer than the mass migration of the late 1940s onwards. This mass migratory movement reached its peak in 1961, when approximately 74,590 entered this country. The year 1961 is significant as being one year prior to the 1962 Commonwealth Immigrants Act, which greatly limited Black immigration from the Caribbean to Britain.[6]

The experience of poor, marginalized, and oppressed peoples within Christian history and the Church has largely been one of struggle, opposition, and invisibility. Black people have often been perceived as problems rather than opportunities. We have been controlled, denigrated, and treated with suspicion. Only in recent history has our presence within White majority Churches been celebrated.[7]

One of the most significant impacts on African Caribbean communities, arising from their ongoing struggles against the seemingly insuperable edifice of racism in Britain, has been the creation of neo-conservative patterns of socialization and their concomitant cultural norms. A number of scholars have written extensively about Black family life and the social and cultural factors that affect Black families and their structure.[8] One of the hidden aspects of Black life and the cultures that reflect these experiences is the sometimes negative factors that exist within Black communities, which are often overlooked or even excused.

One such hidden issue is the sense of rivalry, competition, and conformity that exists within many Black communities. These communities can exert strong patterns of socialization and conformity due to the external factors that have historically oppressed and limited them.[9] There are many Black people who have been accused of not 'really being Black' or not being 'Black enough'.[10] In effect, these are the Black people who have been perceived as 'letting the side down' in terms of their actions and behaviour. Writers such as Victor Anderson have challenged the way in which other Black scholars have perpetuated aspects of this internal conformity by refusing to acknowledge the inherent diversity within Black cultural life in the African Diaspora.[11]

There is the sense that within oppressed and marginalized groups, where racism and poverty are amongst the main factors that define the nature of community, the struggle to maintain a coherent and collectivist stance against a hostile and uncaring world often leads to particular forms of neo-conservative stance regarding such matters as sexual ethics and their resultant social mores. In such contexts, to be perceived as being different or to be seen as different offers a dangerous challenge to the whole community and their notions of what is permissible or acceptable. To be different is potentially to bring shame upon the whole community. The notion of shame remains a very strong regulatory factor in defining the limits of behaviour, identity, and actions within many diaspora African communities.[12]

I have offered a brief microcosm of aspects of the historic underscoring of African Caribbean life and experience in Britain in order to provide a basis on which to investigate the attitudes and theological thinking of a group of Black Caribbean Christians. I am in no way suggesting that the reactions of this group are emblematic of every community of African Caribbean Christians in Britain. Clearly, one would need to undertake a very different mode of theological inquiry in order to amass that sort of data and so make such generic and overarching findings for any group of people.[13]

Rather, in this work, by looking in more detail at one particular group of African Caribbean Christians in Britain, I want to suggest that there are themes and patterns of thought that provide the underscoring of host-societal and attitudinal responses to the phenomenon of HIV/AIDS.

II. Working with the group

The group with whom I worked for this study, initially in the late 1990s and then more recently, is located towards the south west of Birmingham. Birmingham is the second largest city in England. It is a vibrant multiethnic city whose population numbers approximately 1.3 million. The group of African Caribbean Christians with whom I worked were drawn from largely Black majority Methodist, Pentecostal, Anglican, and Reformed Churches in the area. Of the group of twelve, seven had originally travelled to the UK from Jamaica, whilst of the other five three traced their roots to the island of St Kitts and two were from another Caribbean island called Montserrat. I met with the group on three occasions, each meeting lasting approximately two hours.

The first meeting was largely taken up with reminding the group of the previous meeting some seven years ago. Eight of the twelve were veterans from the previous meeting. The five newer members of the group had been chosen by me from a more recent piece of work I had undertaken,[14] whilst others had been invited (with my permission) by existing group members. Subsequent meetings explored the role of God and God's agency in dealing with suffering and disease in the lives of believers and those who would not describe themselves as Christians.

III. Biblical reflections

In order to assist the group in focussing on how they might reflect on the issue of suffering and illness with particular reference to HIV/AIDS, I asked the group to engage with Luke 8: 40–48. This narrative is Luke's account of Jesus' encounter with a woman haemorrhaging.

I split the group of twelve into four groups of three and invited them to reflect on this passage by adopting the persona of a particular character in the narrative. One group became Jesus, the second the woman with the 'issue of blood', the third the disciples, and the fourth the crowd. I invited the group to imagine that they were present as this narrative unfolds and to record their feelings (in character) as the action takes place around them.

Once I had 'set the exercise up', the remainder of the session was spent exploring the text in character. On resumption from the exercise, the groups were de-briefed in order that they could come out of role and would not take any negative or difficult feelings home with them. Finally, immediate feelings, thoughts, and overall reflections were recorded on flip-chart pieces of paper for further analysis in the third and final meeting.

A number of important themes emerged from the different groups as they immersed themselves in character within the framework of the biblical narrative. The main theme that emerged was what I term 'contractual compassion'. In using this term I am referring to the ways in which the group asserted that God's grace and healing for any individual suffering from HIV/AIDS was a direct correlation to how that individual might have contracted the virus in the first instance, and whether they were repentant of their sins.

When the group was asked if it mattered how the sufferer had contracted the virus, nine out of the twelve said yes, so for most in the group it did matter. If the sufferer were known to be gay or lesbian or an intravenous drug user, for example, then this knowledge has a major impact upon their resulting response. Whilst no one in the group displayed a particular hardened response of 'they brought it upon themselves', there was nonetheless, a sense that contracting the HIV virus was the natural corollary of such forms of sinful behaviour. 'If you defy God's law then there are consequences', argued one member of the group.

What is interesting to note is that the reactions of most members of the group were influenced to a great extent by the societal and historico-cultural factors impacting on African Caribbean communities to which reference was made at the beginning of this essay. For most members of the group (all of whom were over fifty)[15] the struggles against racism, marginalization, and societal indifference were such that the means by which many Black Christian communities seek to challenges such systemic ills was through a retreating into themselves, buttressed against such forces by neo-conservative religio-cultural mores and their accompanying theological norms.

Robert Beckford has addressed particular aspects of Black Christianity in Britain and its restrictive self-serving brand of faith that seeks to engage only those who adhere to the religio-cultural norms of the faith community and might describe themselves as being saved.[16] In an earlier work, Beckford analyses the praxis of particular Pentecostal churches in London whose mission theology is unable to bridge the gap between the structural socio-political concerns that exert a disproportionate hold over those on the margins of the church and society and those who are 'saved' within the faith community.[17] People suffering with HIV/AIDS are clearly located as those who through inappropriate behaviour and actions are not saved; for sanctification and holiness would have precluded these forms of actions in the first instance.

When I asked the group to correlate their reflections with the praxis of Jesus and his engagement with the woman in the text, the group were convinced, at least initially, that the woman was an 'innocent sufferer'. Essentially, her plight was not of her making and so Jesus' response of healing her was one that was entirely in keeping with the righteousness of God.

When I challenged the group to reflect on what might be construed as 'deserving and undeserving suffering', i.e. whether any one of us could really deserve God's love and grace, all the members clearly recognized the fault lines in their initial responses. Many recognized that their initial responses were ones coloured by the often restrictive and inhibited cultural norms that they had unconsciously imbibed; which themselves are products of an overarching framework of racism and oppression that has dominated the lives of most Black people living in Britain since the mass post-war migration movements of the mid-part of the last century.[18]

When the group was invited to re-think its initial reactions, it was heartening to see the extent to which uncritical generalized assertions were replaced with a desire to try and understand and respond better.

The group was offered some reflections and thoughts by a number of North American theologians and educators, thinking particularly of the work of Gary Gunderson. Gunderson uses the insights of an interfaith health programme in Atlanta to illustrate how congregations can share ideas and experiences in order to support and be in solidarity with those who are broken and suffering.[19] I have found Gunderson's notion of the church as sanctuary, or a 'safe space' to be particularly apposite in the context of this essay.[20] The notion of the church as safe or hospitable space is one that is utilised in the ecumenical report on children in the church, entitled *Unfinished Business*.[21]

Charles Foster has done much to raise our awareness of the need for congregations to create educational models to assist in the task of trying to construct communities that can handle diversity and conflict in a creative fashion.[22] In a collaborative piece of work with Theodore Brelsford, Foster has undertaken case study research, highlighting the differing (and successful) approaches of a number of churches to engaging with issues of difference, and how plural communities of faith learn how to celebrate their diversity.[23] The challenge that confronted this group was one of how to demonstrate hospitality and inclusivity. How can churches become safe, hospitable spaces where those who are vulnerable and broken can find a welcoming home? In respect to this central defining issue, Foster writes: 'The movement from messages of hostility to hospitality is required for congregations seeking to embrace the strangers they find in their communities. The difference is seen in comparing the posture of the Prodigal Son's father – standing out on the road expectantly waiting – to the posture of the sulking brother, refusing to participate in the banquet.'[24]

The challenge for all of us is to learn to live out the generosity of spirit that is displayed by the father to his son in this famous passage. As this narrative hopefully demonstrates, this generosity is ultimately a gift of grace for it often runs contrary to what we would normally want or choose to do. The members of the group saw this form of praxis as a possibility for themselves as they reflected further on the Lukan passage and their existential engagement with the text and its correlation with contemporary experience.

IV. A Black theological re-reading of Luke 8: 40–48

I was conscious that the group remained wedded to notions of 'contractual compassion'. Whilst they acknowledged the all-embracing and inclusive reality of God's grace in the lives of 'all sinners', I was nevertheless struck by the fact that there remained a sense in which the existence of this abundant grace was one that tolerated particular groups of people rather than celebrating their life and any concomitant experience. In order to push the group to reflect further on this issue I invited them, in the final section of the third meeting, to see how a Black theology reading of this Lukan text might open up new vistas for a renewed and more expansive form of praxis as it pertains to those suffering from HIV/AIDS in Black communities in Britain.

One of the great challenges facing all our Christian faith communities is the challenge of trying to find relevance in the task of reading the Bible. The Bible remains central to the faith of virtually all Black Christians.[25] How can those of us who are charged with leading Bible studies become so energized and inspired that we find new ways of opening up the scriptures for the adults and children we may lead?[26] In this, the final section of this essay, I want to offer a Black theology reading of Luke chapter 8 and demonstrate how a politicized reading of this text can challenge African Caribbean Christian communities to re-think their praxis as it relates to those suffering with HIV/AIDS.

One of the first things to note about Jesus' engagement with the crowd and the woman in the Lukan text is that he is fully engaged in the context in which he is situated. First, Jesus is close to the action. He is within the crowd, not distant from it. Jesus' actions involve being emotionally and physically involved with the context in which he finds himself.[27] This very intentionality of Jesus acts as a counterbalance to the non-contextual and often abstracted theologies of predominantly prosperity-led practitioners of Black Christianity as seen in the likes of Creflo Dollar[28] in the U.S. and Matthew Ashimolowo in the UK.[29] Jesus engages with the context in which he is located, in a real and embodied way, and does not retreat into spiritual banalities as a means of avoiding being labelled 'political'.[30]

Jesus' public engagement eschews any sense of the closed binary of 'them and us' that seems to characterize aspects of the worse forms of self-congratulatory, over-regulated models of holiness-inspired conceptions of Black Church practice and Black Christianity, as a whole, across the African Diaspora.[31]

A Black theological reading of this text is an ideological form of hermeneutical practice that challenges the casual ethnocentric and ecclesiological certainties that belittle, oppress, and marginalize some people over and against others.[32] Such a Black theology re-reading challenges the notions that some people are created more in God's image than others. It challenges those who feel that some people belong more than others. It challenges those who think that some people are a part of the 'us' and others who are different are a part of the 'them'.[33]

For those who think that some belong and deserve to be noticed, like the Jairuses of this world, but that others can and should be ignored because they are unclean or seemingly not worthy, like the woman who was suffering from a blood disease, this text can and should be an immense challenge. In terms of the woman, I read her plight in hermeneutical terms as a Black gay, lesbian, bi-sexual, trans-gendered person or intravenous drug user who is seen as 'beyond the pale' owing to her social condition. Her plight of being on the edge or beyond the pale is one that is recognized by many sufferers with HIV/AIDS in a number of Black communities in Britain. Jesus' actions bring her from the margins into the centre of the action and the narrative. She is affirmed and healed. No questions are asked as to whether she is deserving, or in what contexts she contracted her illness.

A Black-theology-inspired reading of this text, in which Jesus is seen as an inconoclastic disturber of the status quo, challenges us to re-think what we mean by the bounded nature of our theologies that still work on the binaries of 'in' and 'out'. A Black-theology reading suddenly challenges us to reassess who is upset by the 'Good news' of Christ? Is it those who think they are on the inside, in which their cultural taboos are tolerated and affirmed, or those on the so-called outside who suddenly find themselves acceptable and welcomed? For all these people in the former category, a Black-theology re-reading of this text is bad news, because it is a disturber and a denouncer of all that they hold to be true.[34]

A Black-theology reading of this text can open up new ways of seeing established and well-worn patterns and practices. It can challenge hitherto conservative African Caribbean Christian communities to reassess their praxis as it impacts and engages with those struggling with HIV/AIDS in Britain. It can move beyond 'contractual compassion' and 'mere tolerance' to radical affirmation and hospitality, where the first truly become last and the last and the least are made first within the communal practices and ways of being the 'Body of Christ'.

Notes

1. See Anthony G. Reddie, *Acting in Solidarity: Reflections in Critical Christianity*, London: Darton Longman & Todd, 2005, pp. 127–35

2. See Mike Phillips and Trevor Phillips *Windrush: the irresistible rise of multi-racial Britain*, London: HarperCollins, 1999.

3. Selective literature includes R. B. Davidson, *Black British*, Oxford: Oxford University Press, 1966; R. A. Easterlin, *Immigration*, Cambridge, Mass., 1982; Paul Hartman and Charles Hubbard, *Immigration and the Mass Media*, London: Davis-Poynter, 1974; Edward Scobie, *Black Britannia: A history of Blacks in Britain*, Chicago: Johnson Publishing Co, 1972; Ken Pryce, *Endless Pressure*, Bristol: Classical Press, 1979; Winston James and Clive Harris, *Migration, Racism and Identity*, London: Verso, 1993.

4. Ian Duffield, in *History Today*, Vol. 31 (Sept. 1981), p.34.

5. Peter Fryer, *Staying Power: The History of Black People in Britain*, London: Pluto Press, 1984, p.10.

6. Ceri Peach, *West Indian Immigration to Britain*, London: Oxford University Press, 1968, p.82. Documentary evidence attesting to the significant Black presence in Britain in the post-Renaissance period can be found in James Walvin, *Black and White: The Negro and English Society 1555–1945*, London: Allen Lane, 1973; James Walvin, *The Black Presence: A Documentary History of the Negro in England, 1550–1860*, London: Orbach and Chambers, 1971; F. O. Shyllon, *Black People in Britain: 1555–1833*, London: Institute of Race Relations and Oxford University Press, 1977; Douglas A. Lorimer, *Colour, Class and the Victorians*, Leicester: Leicester University Press, 1978. An important biography to note is Mary Seacole's *Wonderful Adventures. Ziggy Alexander and Audrey Dewjee*, London: Falling Wall Press, 1984.

7. The first significant positive sense of my own self-worth within the Methodist Church came with the publication of Heather Walton's *A Tree God Planted: Black People in British Methodism*, London: Ethnic Minorities in Methodism Working Group, The Methodist Church, 1985.

8. See Lee N. June (ed.), *The Black Family*, Grand Rapids, Michigan: Zondervan Publishing, 1991.

9. See Franz Fanon, *The Wretched of the Earth*, New York: Grove Books, 1984.

10. See Isaac Julien 'Black Is, Black Ain't: Notes on De-Essentializing Black

Identities', in Gina Dent (ed.), *Black Popular Culture*, Seattle: Bay Press, 1992, pp. 255–63

11. Victor Anderson, *Beyond Ontological Blackness*, New York: Continuum, 1995.
12. See Edward P. Wimberly, *Moving From Shame to Self-Worth: Preaching and Pastoral Care*, Nashville, Tenn.: Abingdon Press, 1999.
13. In this regard the work of the British Empirical Practical theologian Leslie Francis is particularly apposite. His theological work is explored through the framework of quantitative social science methodologies. See Leslie J. Francis, *Faith and Psychology: personality, religion and the individual*, London: Darton Lomgman & Todd, 2005).
14. See Anthony G. Reddie, *Dramatizing Theologies: A Participative Approach to Black God-talk*, London: Equinox, 2006.
15. The fact that the group was older was very much in keeping with the age demographics of most inner-city Black, African Caribbean congregations in Britain. Many inner-city churches are in effect, ageing congregations.
16. Robert S. Beckford, 'Theology in the Age of Crack: Crack Age, Prosperity Doctrine and "Being There"', in *Black Theology in Britain: A Journal of Contextual Praxis* Vol. 4, No.1 (Nov. 2001), pp. 9–24.
17. Robert Beckford, *Dread and Pentecostal*, London: SPCK, 2000, p. 204.
18. See Anthony G. Reddie, *Nobodies to Somebodies*, Peterborough: Epworth Press, 2003, pp. 3–36
19. See Gary Gunderson, *Deeply Woven Roots: Improving the Quality of Life in Your Community*, Minneapolis: Fortress Press, 1997.
20. *Ibid.*, pp. 83–92
21. *Unfinished Business: Children and the Churches* (Commissioned by the Consultative Group on Ministry among Children – CGMC), London: CCBI Publications, 1995.
22. See Charles R. Foster, *Educating Congregations: The Future of Christian Education*, Nashville, Tenn.: Abingdon, 1994.
23. See Charles R. Foster and Theodore Brelsford, *We Are The Church Together: Cultural Diversity in Congregational Life*, Valley Forge, P.A.: Trinity Press International, 1996.
24. Charles R. Foster *Embracing Diversity: Leadership in Multicultural Congregations*, Herndon, VA: The Alban Institute, 1998, p. 57.
25. See Anthony G. Reddie, 'Editorial' in *Black Theology: An International Journal*, Vol. 4, No.1, London: Equinox: 2006, p. 89.
26. I have attempted something of this sort in terms of my previous work. See Anthony G. Reddie, *Growing into Hope*, 2 vols, Peterborough: The Methodist Publishing House, 1998. See also Anthony G. Reddie, *Nobodies to Somebodies*, *op. cit.*, pp.53–7.
27. See Robert Beckford, 'Theology in the Age of Crack', *art. cit.*
28. See http://www.creflodollarministries.org/ for further details of his ministry.

29. See http://www.kicc.org.uk/ for further details of his ministry.

30. See Robert Beckford 'Theology in the Age of Crack', *art. cit.*

31. I have addressed elements of this phenomenon in a previous piece of work. See Anthony G. Reddie, *Acting in Solidarity*, *op. cit.*

32. See Harry H. Singleton, III, *Black Theology and Ideology*, Collegeville, Mn: The Liturgical Press, 2002, pp. 47–67; see also Anthony B. Pinn and Dwight N. Hopkins (eds.), *Loving The Body*, New York: Palgrave Macmillan, 2006, for an excellent exploration of the limits placed on Black people by the Black church in terms of its prohibitions around same-gender sexual relationships and sexuality as a whole.

33. This form of reading has been inspired by Kelly Brown Douglas' recent book *What's Faith Got to Do With It?*, Maryknoll, NY: Orbis, 2005, where Brown challenges the traditional Christian imperial hegemony that is built on an adversarial closed monotheism.

34. This has been the central task of Black theologians such as James Cone and Womanists such as Jacquelyn Grant, both of whom have a strong christological focus to their theological method. See James H. Cone, *God of the Oppressed*, San Francisco: HarperSanFrancisco, 1975, pp. 108–95. See also See Jacquelyn Grant, *White Women's Christ and Black Women's Jesus*, Atlanta: Scholar's Press, 1989.

The HIV/AIDS Scenario in India:
Prevention of Mother-to-child Transmission in
a Rural District of South India

N. M. SAMUEL

Background

The first case of AIDS was discovered in India in 1986. Since then the number of cases has increased dramatically, and the present number is 5.7 million. India has overtaken South Africa in the estimates of the number of HIV-infected in the country. In 2006 we reflected on the twenty-five years since the first cases were reported by the CDC in the USA, and it was a time when we pondered on our own epidemic – its dynamics, the preventive strategies adopted, their strengths and weaknesses.

We have been involved in HIV/AIDS work since the early 1990s. As a medical university our concern was to impart information to our faculty and students. Whenever we talked about HIV/AIDS we could only say it lead to death as there were no appropriate drugs that could be used in public health settings. When we discussed prevention it was only condom use. In 1995 it was shown that transmission of HIV can be prevented from an infected mother to infant through AZT (076 study) being given to a seropositive pregnant woman. This was good news, and we embarked upon using AZT (with some modifications) with rural pregnant women who were HIV infected.

At the same time we were receiving letters from the general practitioners in a small rural district informing us that they were observing HIV/AIDS cases in their practices and wanted us to assist with the confirmation of the diagnosis. This led us to go to this rural district to further investigate. A student undertook a survey to observe the seropositivity among pregnant women in Namakkal, and the seropositivity was 6%. This startled us into going back to undertake further surveys. At the same time our group was examining the number of seropositive pregnant women in the metropolitan city of Chennai in four large public institutions. The prevalence of seropositivty was less than 1%. It was clear that HIV prevalence is clustered. We have learnt that there were differences in prevalence over various parts of the country and what one observed in one district was not necessarily the same in another.

Introduction

Namakkal district is situated 400 kms from Chennai city, and the only way to reach Namakkal is by bus or car. It is like a land-locked district and can be reached by road alone. The inhabitants of the district are mostly long-distance truck drivers and agricultural workers. There is a high rate of migration of men and women in search of work. Most of the individuals in Namakkal are rural and most of them are partly educated, while others have primary schooling. This is the first rural prevention of mother-to-child transmission (PMTCT) centre established in India.

Description: Prevention of Mother-to-child transmission centre – Namakkal

In 2000 we established a PMTCT centre in Namakkal district government hospital and the following services continue to be provided:

- Voluntary counselling and testing;
- Provision of confidential counselling following informed consent
- Offer of antiretroviral prophylaxis – AZT and NVP
- Home-based care
- Breast feeding options
- Family Planning

This report is related to our experiences in establishing a rural centre to prevent HIV transmission from mother to child, what we have observed, and what we have learned. In particular ethical issues faced will be highlighted in this report.

Voluntary counselling and testing

Most of the pregnant women who seek antenatal services are young women in their early twenties. These women are counselled in a group-counselling session that precedes clinical documentation. They are counselled on nutrition, sexually-transmitted infections, and HIV/AIDS. Pregnant women go to hospitals to confirm pregnancy and to learn if the infant is normal. Several women after their initial visit do not return for follow-up till the time of delivery, while some keep to their monthly appointments. Women bear the burden of the family, in that they have to take care of the home and continue to go out to work and bring money to live. Therefore they find it difficult to travel to the clinic as they will lose a daily wage that is important for their survival. So we set up five clinics close to their homes in different locations. These were welcomed by the community. To the present 29,789 women have been counselled and tested. Of these, 29,649 (99.5%) were tested using rapid tests, and 519 tested HIV-positive (1.75%).

Women wait to receive the results and 98% of them receive the test results. Following counselling sessions we often wonder how many of them truly understand the disease process and the sequelae.

Provision of confidential counselling following informed consent

Informed consent is obtained prior to testing. The written consent is in the local language and the counsellors explain to the women in detail before obtaining their consent.

This poses a considerable dilemma in that we often are not sure whether women understand the consent they have just provided. The consent is for testing and, if tested HIV-positive, to receive drugs as antiretroviral prophylaxis. Following the test results, if detected to be positive, we counsel them individually and often with the client's consent counsel the partner and a family member who is responsible for the care of the infected individual. This is what we term 'shared confidentiality' – a term used in the resource-limited settings. We continue to protect the individual's right but modified to suit the local situation and particularly in the cultural context. There is, however, danger in this approach as some of them may misuse the information!

Offer of antiretroviral prophylaxis – AZT and NVP

Initially we administered AZT, a single drug, for longer periods and then switched to short-course therapy (with AZT) as was recommended. This was followed by a single dose of Nevirapine to the mother and a single dose to the infant within three days after birth – the standard care in developing countries. We are also aware that single-dose Nevirapine may produce resistance to the drug and if this happens in women then their future use of this drug in combination therapy is compromised.

The dilemma is between what we know and what we are not sure of and how much information has to be provided to the client! We know that the antiretroviral drugs used as prophylaxis do provide protection to between 45 and 65%. How to translate this to a rural woman who looks to the health-care worker to provide magic bullets and magic answers to her problems?

Home-based care

We have observed that most of our clients do not return to the hospital for follow-up treatment. The reasons are: long distances to the hospital; loss of a daily wage; long waits to get on a bus; the unfriendly nature of some of the health-care providers; and the stigma associated with attending a HIV/AIDS centre – the list could go on and on!

We have learned that undertaking home visits makes the women much more at ease with issues that were uppermost on their minds, but the health-care settings were not conducive to them to interact. We learned that counselling is not a one-time issue but a process that needs to be provided to the women again and again. They appreciate that they can ask questions and are able to discuss the issues relating to their partners and the feeding practices and options of the infant with ease. Home-based visits also enable health-care workers to undertake 'pill counts' and find out if another member of the family is sharing their medicines – a problem often observed in our programmes, particularly when more than one member in a family is HIV-infected. The ethical dilemma that is faced is confidentiality and identity when the health-care worker visits the woman at home. There is a likelihood of the neighbours knowing why a health-care worker often visits a particular family. This leads to stigmatization within a community. We have tried several ways to mask the identity of the health-care workers, but in vain. The vehicles were parked away from the home of the woman, and no uniforms were used by the staff.

Breast feeding options

Breast feeding is another route by which HIV can be transmitted from mother to the new-born infant. While in developed nations breast feeding is often not advocated and breast-milk substitutes are the norm, it is not advisable to follow a similar practice in rural India. Breast-milk substitutes are advocated in urban India depending upon the economic status of the families. So the standard practice in our clinics is for mothers to make a choice – to breast feed or not to breast feed. After the counselling session the majority of mothers agree not to breast feed their infants. It is the desire of every mother to provide the best for the infant, and this norm persuades them not to breast feed. They practise this strategy for the initial month or two and then find that it's impossible for them to continue this method as it's expensive. So they resort to mixed feeds using unclean water that cause more damage to the infant and probably enhance HIV transmission.

We are aware that this is the reality in resource-limited settings, but we are 'uncomfortable' at having to use differential strategies that are based on economics.

Family Planning

India's population is 1.2 billion and will probably overtake China in the next three decades to become the world's most populous nation. For the poor, children are an asset, their parents' social security. With this pride, most women wish to have more children and are reluctant to space them. It is also to be understood that they are not sure whether the new-born will live to see her/his fifth birthday!

So intense counselling is undertaken to persuade young mothers to space their children. At times we feel this is a losing battle, but we carry on, resolved that fewer healthy children are a pride of a family.

Some mothers wish to terminate pregnancies after knowing the facts that HIV can be transmitted from mother to infant and via breast milk. It is a dilemma whether to counsel them to terminate or not to. But we are also aware that all the current regimens are in practice not 100% effective. So the ethical dilemma for the health-care provider is: What is the right message I should give the mother?

At times the mothers ask the counsellors and the doctors what we would do if we were in that situation! Life needs to be protected, and there are preventive strategies that can support life.

Conclusion

HIV/AIDS infects the most sexually active age groups. Death may occur over the next five to ten years. With other infections, such as tuberculosis, death may come even faster. We in India need to mount an effective response to three epidemics: the HIV/AIDS epidemic, the Tuberculosis epidemic, and the third equally important epidemic of stigma and discrimination. *We all need to act now to prevent these epidemics and to protect future generations from HIV/AIDS*

Life-affirming African Theological Reflection on HIV and AIDS

ISABEL APAWO PHIRI

Introduction

After twenty-three years of HIV and AIDS, the Church in Africa has struggled to come up with a theology to meet the challenge. The major contributing factor is the Church's lack of a theology of sexuality in the context where 99 per cent of HIV infections in Sub-Saharan Africa are through unprotected heterosexual relationships. While the traditional African societies, for example the Chewa of Malawi, had their own institutionalized ways of teaching and talking about sexuality, the coming of modernization and Christianity undermined these traditional systems without offering an alternative. Furthermore, our theological institutions have not sufficiently equipped the church leaders to come up with a theology of HIV and AIDS and a theology of sexuality that is life-affirming and takes the African world-view into account. It is not surprising therefore that many church leaders still consider HIV and AIDS as God's judgment on people for sexual sins without giving a theological explanation as to why many people who are practising unlawful sexual intercourse do not have HIV and AIDS or many women who are practising lawful sex are HIV positive. It is the aim of this paper to attempt an African theological reflection on HIV and AIDS.

I. The Circle and HIV and AIDS: a gender-based response

From the outset it is very important that I locate myself so that the reader understands what is influencing my theological reflection on this topic. I locate myself within African women theologies as propagated by the Circle of Concerned African Women theologians (hereafter, the Circle). African women theologies belong to a wider family of feminist theology, which is further categorized as liberation theology. Both theologies are different varieties of Christian theology and they acquired their names on the basis of context and approach. On the African continent, we have a number of liberation theologies. The African Christian women have called their reflection of the African context and the Christian faith African women theologies.

Why theologies and not just theology? The word theologies is used in its plural form because African women theologians want to acknowledge the fact that even within Africa there is diversity of women's experiences due to differences in race, culture, politics, economy, and religions. Despite the differences in terminology, all women would like to see the end of sexism in their lives and the establishment of a more just society of men and women that seek the well-being of the other. They seek justice for all the oppressed including the environment.

African women theologies examine the issues of resurrection, to include restoration of the present life from death-promoting activities. They want to see the Jesus of the Gospels who healed to bring healing in today's world that is polluted with HIV and AIDS. African women theologians have chosen to make HIV and AIDS the main issue for their theology from 2002 to 2007. This is the Circle's contribution to the Ecumenical movement's response to HIV and AIDS in Africa.

The Circle has highlighted the centrality of gender and HIV and AIDS. Philippe Denis has rightly said that 'HIV and AIDS is ultimately a gender issue'.[1] This statement is supported by the fact that, according to Sally Baden and Heike Wach, the major mode of transmission in Sub-Saharan Africa is through heterosexual intercourse, with marriage as the major risk factor for any African woman to contract the HIV virus'.[2] This has been echoed by the Hunger Project, which has stated: 'Sub-Saharan Africa is the only region in the world in which more women than men are infected with HIV – 55 per cent of infected adults are women. Teenage girls in Sub-Saharan Africa are five times more likely to be infected than boys.'[3]

The statement that this paper is making is that, if we do not deal with gender and HIV, the world will not make a difference in combating the virus. Therefore we need to address the fact that physiological differences, social and cultural norms, and economic and power relations between women and men have a very big impact in the process of who gets infected, how one can prevent infection, and who looks after the sick.

African women theologians' writings have shown that in Africa marriage is at the centre of the African community.[4] Yet marriage is also the centre of patriarchy, which constructs the subordinate position of African women. This position does not work well in the era of HIV and AIDS, when research shows that there are more new infections of HIV among married women than any other group.[5] It has been argued by the World Health Organization that the major reason why this is the case is 'the sexual and economic subordination of women'.[6] Articles in two of the Circle's publications, *The Will to Arise* (1992) and *Violence Against Women* (1995), have described very clearly the subordinate positions of women in Africa. As long as women continue to be put in subordinate positions through biblical teachings and African cultural practices, it will be difficult to control HIV and AIDS in Africa. Yet the Western world has shown that HIV and AIDS are manageable, controllable, and preventable.

Women are also carers of those infected with HIV and AIDS, and they take care of the orphans with minimum economic and social support. HIV and AIDS have brought us to a theology of praxis that looks at all of us as agents of change to promote life.

African women theologians have also agreed that research into religious, cultural, and social practices that make women vulnerable to HIV and AIDS is not a sufficient contribution. The African women theologians have taken upon themselves the task of engagement with the community to save lives. The Circle has entered into partnership with Ecumenical HIV and AIDS Initiatives in Africa (EHAIA) to work with Churches and theological institutions in Africa to streamline HIV and AIDS.

II. A challenge for a new theology

First and foremost, the creation of a new theology that deals with HIV and AIDS needs to deal with issues of sexuality in the African worldview. African societies celebrate sexuality. Before the coming of Western civilization to Africa, African communities had different occasions on which sexuality was celebrated. Among the Chewa of Malawi, this was done through the different levels of initiation ceremonies for boys and girls, women and men.[7] After the arrival of Christianity in Malawi, discussions on human sexuality became an embarrassment to the Church. It is not surprising then that in the context of HIV and AIDS, the Church is struggling with discussions of sexuality. The message that this gives out is that from a Christian perspective, anything to do with sex is sinful. Silence in the Church on discussion of sexuality, therefore, is not as a result of African culture but a new culture that has evolved as a result of African interaction with Christianity and Western civilization. This cannot be a biblically-founded message as it contradicts God's message that everything that God created for humanity was good. It is therefore the task of the Church to reclaim the celebration of sexuality as part of human wholeness in a world that is broken by HIV and AIDS.

Second, a mission-oriented theology of HIV and AIDS acknowledges that the Bible is central in Africa and is used as an authoritative book of the Church.[8] Whenever the Church is seeking direction, the Bible is consulted in all circumstances. Musa Dube has rightly stated that it is therefore not surprising that in the era of the HIV and AIDS pandemic, the Church has gone back to the Bible to search for knowledge on the disease, healing, stigma and isolation, guilt and fear, caring, death and dying.[9] African theology has shown the similarities between the Old Testament and African beliefs and practices. In African religion, individual sins affect the whole community.[10] This may explain why the Church's initial and to some extent current response to HIV and AIDS is that they were/are as a result of a person's sins and that God was punishing the people involved.[11] This approach promoted the HIV and AIDS stigma and prevented the Church from reaching out in mission to the affected and infected. Therefore Africa is now exploring new ways of reading and interpreting the Bible that helps the Church to move away from a theology of HIV and AIDS as a punishment from God to a theology of God who is in solidarity with the HIV- and AIDS-affected and infected people in the same way that liberation theologies have depicted God to be on the side of the poor and the marginalized. God, Jesus Christ, and the Church in Africa are being described as the ones with HIV and AIDS. Therefore it is the whole Church that needs to embrace messages of protection from HIV and healing from AIDS.

Third, HIV and AIDS are also making African women theologians revisit the question of why human beings suffer. I agree with Musimbi Kanyoro, who has stated that, 'to do theology in Africa today is to do theology among a people with much suffering. There is so much death on our continent that reality makes a mockery of the bravery of Job, the biblical giant of tribulations'.[12]

HIV and AIDS have just added to the intensity of suffering on the continent. There is suffering that is caused by rejection when people reveal their status. There is also suffering due to lack of medication when they are due to be on treatment. There is suffering of family members resulting from lack of resources or from being overworked in the process of looking after the sick and orphans. There is the suffering experienced by widows and orphans. African women agree that suffering is part of human life and it should not necessarily be interpreted as a result of sin. What is sinful is to accept unjust systems that cause people to suffer unnecessarily. This calls for a theology that names the unjust systems and works towards life-affirming systems.

Fourth, the issue of HIV and AIDS is also connected to conceptions of life. The theology of creation as depicted in Genesis 1–2 shows what is in God's plan for the sacredness of all life. There is interdependency and goodness of creation. Sex becomes a gift which is wholesome and to be enjoyed by the created order. The same image is depicted in African creation myths. God's image is found in both men and women. We also need to acknowledge that the world of HIV and AIDS is a broken world, as in Genesis 3, in which quality of life does not exclude suffering. However, in the conception of quality of life in the time of HIV and AIDS, the protection of life should be uppermost. African women are aware that (even in the Church) couples are not remaining faithful to one another, despite the Church's constant message of abstaining and being faithful. Therefore, while we are sorting out our power-games of patriarchy and the sanctity of marriage as originally intended by God, human life has to be protected. The experience of the majority of African women has shown that life cannot be protected by prayer alone. One has to apply wisdom as given by God and act to save life. The process of acting requires a re-examination of the Church's teachings about marriage, sexuality, and divorce. Marriage is a place where lawful sex takes place. However, this has also proved to be a death-trap in the context of HIV and AIDS. African theology on marriage should include making lawful sex be safe for those involved. This can only happen if the Church deals with issues of gender justice.

Fifth, HIV and AIDS have also raised the issue of corporate sin that calls for all people to re-examine their private and public life in order to protect life. It does not make sense that one part of humanity can have a good quality of life even after infection with HIV, while the other half dies quickly due to poverty and curable opportunist infections. This is where the message of Jesus in Luke 4.18–19 becomes the mission of the Church to deal with all forms of oppression, which include social injustice, disease, poverty, and racial and sexual discrimination, and to promote liberation, social justice, life, and healing. We need a prophetic theology to come from the Church to guide the rest of society on how to deal with these difficult issues of justice for all children of God.

Lastly, healing was central in the mission of Jesus and it is important in African religion. This explains why the churches that have adopted physical healing are very popular in Africa. In such churches, Jesus is the Healer. Desperate cases of people with AIDS are taken to these churches for healing.

Despite the fact that many people who are critically ill die at the churches, people do not lose hope in a God who is a healer. They still go to church in droves to seek Jesus the healer. Jesus becomes their last hope. They hope for physical healing. Hope in Jesus as healer is what gives them the motivation to face another day even up to their deathbed. They cling to hope for healing. This is where sensitive pastoral counselling is needed. A church that is competent to deal with HIV and AIDS knows that the healing of Jesus cannot be limited to physical healing. It is wholesome so that even in death one finds healing.

Conclusion

The major argument of this article is that HIV and AIDS should force the Church in Africa to re-examine its theology about sexuality and the relationship between men and women. I have used the theoretical framework of African women theologians to show that the Church needs to take gender seriously when theologizing about HIV and AIDS, as it has been identified as one major element that is fuelling HIV and AIDS in Africa. It has also shown that Church needs to celebrate sexuality in its wholeness within a broken world. In its mission on HIV and AIDS, the Church needs to take the Bible as central to the people's understanding of disease and healing. However, it is a liberative hermeneutics that should be central when using the Bible in the context of HIV and AIDS. This article has also shown that the messages of abstaining and being faithful are not enough in the prevention of HIV. One has to seek wisdom from God in using comprehensive HIV-prevention methods. The guiding principle should be the sacredness of life that needs to be protected at all times by everyone. This requires a prophetic theology that transforms oppressive structures in the Church and society in order to protect life. I have also acknowledged the importance of a theology of healing, which is central in the African world view. However, the concept of healing must be understood in its comprehensive nature so that it is not limited to physical healing alone.

Notes

1. P. Denis, 'Sexuality and AIDS in South Africa', in *Journal of Theology for Southern Africa*, 115 (March, 2003), p. 75.
2. S. Baden and H. Wach, *Gender, HIV AND AIDS transmission and impact: A review of issues and evidence*, Brighton: Institute of Development Studies, 1998, p. 7.

3. Hunger Project, 2001, p. 1.
4. For example see Mercy Amba Oduyoye *Daughters of Anowa: African Women and Patriarchy*, Maryknoll, NY: Orbis, 1995, Ch.6, on marriage and patriarchy, pp. 131–53.
5. G. van Woudenberg, 1998: 8.
6. G. Pieterson, 1996: xi.
7. See I. A. Phiri, *Women, Presbyterianism and Patriarchy: Religious Experiences of Chewa Women in Central Malawi*. Blantyre: CLAM, 1997.
8. Sam Oleka, 'The Authority of the Bible in the African Context', in Samuel Ngewa, Mark Shaw, and Tite Tieno (eds), *Issues in African Christian Theology*, Nairobi: East African Educational Publishers Ltd, 1998, pp. 75–103.
9. Dube, *op. cit.*, 2003, p. 224.
10. Stuart C. Bate, OMI, 'Responsible Healing in a World of HIV and AIDS' in Stuart Bate, OMI (ed.) *Responsibility in the Time of AIDS: A Pastoral Response by Catholic Theologians and AIDS Activists in Southern Africa*. Pietermaritzburg: Cluster Publications, 2003, pp. 158–9.
11. Dorothy Scarborough, 'HIV and AIDS: The Response of the Church', in *Journal of Constructive Theology*, Vol. 7, no. 1 (July 2001), pp. 3–16.
12. Musimbi Kanyoro, *Introducing Feminist Cultural Hermeneutics: An African Perspective*, Sheffield: Sheffield Academic Press, 2002, p. 24.

Obituary

BEATRICE WERE

In 1991 my husband Francis died of AIDS. Four months later I was diagnosed with HIV and my life changed for ever. Francis knew he was positive but had not told me. Like most Ugandan men, he wanted a 'pure' wife, and he got one, for all the good it did me. I had abstained and remained faithful, but ultimately it was meaningless. And so I was left at twenty-two, widowed with two baby daughters, and enveloped by a cloud of bitterness that took years to disperse. My personal story is typical of the way most African women contract HIV. In Africa, 60 per cent of new infections are in women, and many of them are married.

Fifteen years on, I am a long-term survivor. But I know that I am lucky. I have a university degree and a profession to fall back on. As a trained social worker I understand how systems work and have personal and professional support networks to back me. Anti-retroviral drugs supplied by my employer, ActionAid, keep me alive. Unfortunately for many poor women AIDS still kills, while the prejudice and stigma that surround the disease are a life sentence. Africa has already lost a generation to AIDS. Without action, it will lose another. HIV is a matter of life and death, not just for individuals, but for a continent.

It is also an issue of human rights. AIDS is not just an illness of the body. It is an illness of society. On the journey from healthy family woman to HIV-positive single mother, the obstacles are varied and hurtful. Like many women I had to fight a traditional widows' inheritance system where I was supposed to marry my husband's youngest brother, and where my property was claimed by his family.

There was a time when Uganda was heralded for stemming and reversing the rise in its HIV infections. Now, the United Nation's latest AIDS figures show that this is no longer true. The response of the Ugandan Government has shifted from pragmatic to moralistic and, as UNAIDS showed last week, HIV prevalence in women has grown by 2 per cent and in some rural hotspots by as much as 25 per cent

It wasn't that long ago that the Ugandan approach was a classic 'ABC' model – abstinence, being faithful, using a condom. In my case, I settled for 'A' and 'B', which ultimately proved not enough. Yet the three-step policy, while far from perfect, was at least realistic in promoting the use of condoms, which used to be advertised all over Uganda on huge billboards.

Now, under the influence of US donors, often driven by the evangelical right, billboards have been replaced by marches of virgins and proposals for university scholarships for those who remain 'untainted'. A new wave of stigma has overtaken the country; people who are living with HIV are defined as 'loose'. Civil society, the backbone of any approach to defeat AIDS, has become divided in the scramble for US grants.

America's AIDS funding for Uganda is undoubtedly generous. It amounts to $15bn over five years. But its prevention approach, mainly restricting condom distribution to so-called 'high risk' groups such as commercial sex workers and truck drivers, ignores the reality of the African epidemic, which is young and female

We know that girls and young women who stay in education are much less likely to contract the disease. They are more likely to reject patriarchal norms and stand up for their rights, including their right not to have sex. They are less likely to have sex for money, and crucially they are more likely to use a condom when they do have sex.

Assuming it has taken you six minutes to read this, seventy-two people will have died from AIDS around the world and eighty-five have become infected. The response from African governments and the international community must be injected with a dose of realism. G8 countries have promised to fund treatment for those who need it – but no plans are in place. When and if this funding reaches countries like Uganda, there needs to be a fundamental shift in attitudes toward sex and the rights of women, if we are ever to defeat this devastating pandemic.

II. The Discourse in Moral Theology

Is AIDS a Divine Punishment? Excessive Metaphysical Interpretations of a Biological Phenomenon

FRANK SANDERS

'Church marriages can be annulled by the Catholic Church if one of the two partners was suffering from AIDS or was merely HIV-positive when they were married.'[1]

This report appeared in the *Stuttgarter Zeitung* of 21 March 1996 under the headline 'Marriages annulled because of AIDS?' and is said to represent the opinion of Massimo Mingardi – an 'expert in canon law – expressed during a lecture given at a canon-law event in Modena. The mere fact of being infected with the HI-virus when married in church is said to be enough to make a marriage null and void, because the infected person would endanger the partner's life during sex, and that would be immoral. Even though this does not exhaust all aspects of the range of questions in canon law raised by the topic of 'marriage and HIV/AIDS', the report does serve as an introduction to the complex of problems which – long before Mingardi's remarks – were discussed in canon-law circles and finally came to a head in the problem of whether the natural right to marry must be called in question by the existence of an HIV-infection or of a case of AIDS. Certainly, the marriage of HIV-positives and AIDS-patients can be annulled by an ecclesiastical court, but the ground for annulment in such cases cannot be directly associated with the infection, in the sense that the marriage would be null and void *only because* one partner or both partners was already HIV-positive when the church wedding was celebrated. The nullity of a marriage cannot be based on HIV-specific grounds.[2] Mingardi's

51

ideas as cited above apparently caused considerable controversy in Italy, to the extent that even figures on the official side decided that they had to distance themselves from this viewpoint. Accordingly, Cardinal Ersilio Tonini was reported as saying that it was possible to catch HIV through blood transfusions quite *innocently*. Therefore the infected person could not be denied the right to marriage. Although the outcome of the Cardinal's assertion might well be correct, the reasoning behind it is highly question-able. Assessments of the effects of HIV and AIDS on canonical marriage-ability are indeed to be found in the canon-law literature in relation to actual cases. Nevertheless – in respect of entitlement to the fundamental right to marry (cf. can. 1058 CIC) – we often come across the statement that some people have caught the HI-virus *innocently*. This shows how powerfully effective previous judgements (prejudices indeed) can be once they have been made, since the mention of innocent victims inescapably reveals the implicit conviction that some victims must be guilty.

This article neither seeks to cover questions that belong specifically with-in the bounds of canon law and are almost exclusively confined to the complex of problems associated with marital law, nor to examine the current debate on the ethical aspects of HIV/AIDS. Here I am much more con-cerned with the initial period of that discussion, when judgements were expressed that tended to set the future course of reflection on the subject. Their effects on subsequent controversy (both within the Church and among scholars and specialists) are scarcely to be underestimated. For some time now, it seems, they have been influential even in contexts outside the strict confines of the theological disciplines.

More than two decades have passed since the discovery of the HI-virus. We realize now that the speed with which medicine was able to illuminate the obscurity of a hitherto unknown disease was truly impressive. Hardly one year separated the publication of the first cases of the new syndrome from its definition. The news of Robert Gallo's discovery of HIV on 23 April 1984 faced the world with one of the greatest challenges of the twentieth century. At first sight, when treated as a theological topic, a disease would seem to come within the specialized scope of pastoral theology and, in particular, the area of pastoral care of the sick, although it might be said to be of interest primarily to specialists in medical ethics and bio-ethics. Of course, AIDS raises an extremely wide range of theological questions, since it soon became a metaphor for guilt, fear, sin, and death. In fact, AIDS has become a challenge for theologians.

If we try to summarize the various aspects of theological discourse on the subject, we may say, in a quite general sense, that theological discussion of AIDS was concerned with the question of *right and wrong behaviour* in view of the *individual* and *social* threat posed by the immune-deficiency sickness caused by HIV. Accordingly, moral philosophers and moral theologians in particular determined theological reflections on the theme of 'AIDS', which on the one hand looked at the behaviour of healthy people towards those infected, and on the other hand considered the behaviour of the victims in relation to their environment. Although theologians also saw the relevance of socio-ethical and individual-ethical aspects as a whole as a topic requiring investigation, at first HIV and AIDS remained primarily matters for examination from the viewpoint of sexual ethics. Since the appearance of syphilis as an epidemic in the sixteenth century, the human race had not been afflicted by a disease with such an immense influence on its sex life. It is as if some theological authors saw a chance of finding a new audience and reviving a set of topics that had become rather old-hat since the lively discussion at the time of the 'sexual revolution' and *Humanae Vitae*. It seems that they also saw the possibility of taking advantage of the fear associated with sex since the advent of AIDS, and of using it to attack sexual indulgence in the form of promiscuity and permissiveness, and of the social recognition of unmarried and same-sex partnerships. That it was possible for the theme of 'HIV and AIDS' to receive this extraordinary degree of attention from theologians is due to the fact that across the world AIDS was not considered primarily as a terminal illness, but as the result and manifestation of moral disorder with regard to individual or group behaviour – or, more precisely, as the result and manifestation of moral disorder with regard to sexual behaviour. At all events, the fact that the deadly HI-virus was spread mainly through sexual intercourse provided a phenomenal association of sex, morals, and death that appeared powerfully, indeed almost magically, attractive to theologians; or – as Mieth puts it – drew theologians who swarmed about it 'like moths round a light bulb'; or, in scriptural terms: 'Wherever there is a dead body, there the vultures will flock' (Matt. 24.28).'[3]

Initially, the patients requiring treatment were exclusively homosexual men. This led to the view that the community was facing a new immun-odeficiency disease restricted to the homosexual population, which was called GRID (gay related immunodeficiency disease). Talk of the 'gay plague' or 'queer cancer' soon showed who was being labelled as the guilty parties. There was a desire to see AIDS as the logical consequence of sexual misbehaviour. Some people treated AIDS as so speak a punishment for an immoral life. Talk of 'divine punishment' or – with less religious bias – of 'nature's revenge' had an important psychological function for healthy people, for it served to assuage their fear of their own infection and death. Because homosexuality, promiscuity, prostitution, and drug addiction were cited as causes of AIDS, all those who shunned any such 'immoral' and 'abominable' modes of behaviour could think of themselves as in the safe zone, although that meant that those infected by HIV or suffering from AIDS were cast into outer darkness.

When the initial silence of the Churches – with a few exceptions – was broken for the first time, because state-initiated enlightenment campaigns led to quite open and public discussion of the taboo topic of sex, and priority was given simultaneously to recommending condoms as a means of protection from infection, the Churches probably even increased the emphasis on discrimination. By presenting themselves initially as the collective guardian of a strict sexual morality, they helped to encourage speculation about a somehow natural association of guilt, sin, and AIDS, so that 'even today many Christians all over the world do not think primarily of illness in connection with HIV/Aids, but of sin, moral failure, and promiscuity. The result was and remains the attribution of guilt to, the stigmatization of, and discrimination in regard to those affected, and rendering the question taboo.'[4]

Because the nature of the primary mode of transmission of the disease very soon led to the assertion that there was a connection between 'unhealthy' behaviour (since it endangered oneself and others) and 'immoral' conduct,[5] the illness AIDS was directly associated with sin. It was only a short step from there to the classification of AIDS as a punishment from above for abnormal sexual behaviour and drug addiction. When comparing social reactions to classic instances of disease in the past, on the one hand, with those to AIDS, on the other hand, Antihero duly identifies a recurrent social phenomenon: a 'refusal . . . to accept the natural origin of biological events, and a consequent tendency to interpret them using meta–empirical categories'[6] The approach revealed in ecclesiastical and theological discourse about AIDS – that is, the stressing of its function as a 'divine rod of correction' – is yet another example of a far from unfamiliar readiness to revert to an archaic, and emphatically mythological, concept of the religious phenomenon.

In the German-speaking world, Johannes Gründel was one of the first representatives of theological circles to combat this mechanism and decisively to contradict the interpretation of AIDS as God's punishment or a divine scourge, pointing out that it is especially questionable to advance any such interpretation if the victims have been infected in the course of sexual behaviour. Any such explanation disregards the biblical message of God's mercy and of the liberation of creation from suffering, sin, and death. People who talk like that turn the good news into threat and menace, instrumental-ize God as the guarantor of their own notions of morality, and thereby say more about themselves, their idea of values, and their personal image of God than about the God of Christian proclamation.[7] These attempts to explain HIV/AIDS surely originate more in human speculation than in the will of the God who unmistakably revealed himself as pure love. Statements such as the following are surely products more of human than of divine logic: 'God is merciful and patient and calls on sinners to change their ways. If they do not so, then the unremittingly logical outcome is the punishment which in itself represents yet another summons to repent. Therefore we may see punishment as a divine revelation aimed at sinners.'[8]

Eid probably had statements like this in mind when he duly remarked of attempts to use AIDS as an example of divine punishment: 'Any such judge-ment not only has to be rejected totally on theological grounds alone but must be exposed on moral grounds as a manifestation of a compulsive long-ing for vengeance and to punish others, and of an unrelenting demand for expiation. "Look, people are doing dreadful things with impunity! Quite without inhibition, so it seems, they are pandering to their lascivious desires and indulging their whims, inclinations and addictions. This behaviour cannot go unpunished. They must suffer for their sins." This kind of authoritarian mentality betrays a self-righteous wish to control the way other people behave.'[9]

The mere fact that newborn children, haemophiliacs, doctors, nursing staff, and carers have been infected has to make talk of AIDS as a divine punishment totally ludicrous. Moreover, quite early on it was observed that not only homosexuals and drug addicts 'caught' the deadly virus; that heterosexual intercourse was no less hazardous as a mode of transmission;[10] that risky behaviour also allowed the virus to be passed on to marriage part-ners; and, similarly, that it did not hesitate to infect 'innocent' children. The virus is indifferent to skin colour, gender, or sexual orientation. But any argument along these lines failed to impress all those who sought to make not the individual but society as a whole the scapegoat. They found simply everyone responsible, and consequently even 'innocent' victims of the AIDS epidemic were guilty. Meves offers an especially insidious line of argument: 'Most of these disturbed people are not active sinners, but victims of sins generally typical of the times in a secularized society intent on denaturing itself. Their sickness is truly a consequence of their fathers and forefathers having run after false gods, the idols of materialism and egotism, for instance, so that these evildoings are duly visited on the children of sinners down to the third and fourth generations.'[11] It was surely statements like this that Kramer had in mind when he quite rightly said in respect of the different theories of punishment: 'When people bombard others with pronouncements as crazy as this, you often feel that you are not merely listening to ideological maxims but observing psychotic syndromes.'[12] Even if HIV and AIDS were not always directly characterized as divine punishments, the virus and disease syndrome were often stepped up metaphysically by interpreting them as symptoms of a 'prodromal spiritual immunodeficiency'[13] – as a portent in syndrome form intended to urge human beings to penetrate to the root causes of the problem and to tackle the real causes of the sickness.[14] In this sense, Cottier, too, wished to interpret the disease as a sign of the times, 'in so far as it has helped to reveal the far-reaching disorders of our society that represent a threat to human sexuality and true love. . . . There has never been an age when morality and received standards of behaviour have achieved more than a modest average of attainment. But a distinctive characteristic of the current permissive ideology is people's lack of any awareness of sin, and the way in which sexuality and everything to do with handing on the gift of life has been rendered trivial. This new disease forces us to see this situation as it really is.'[15] Is it really possible to interpret AIDS, even if not as a direct divine punishment, at least as a painfully distressing warning signal from God? Buttiglione pointed out that both Jewish prophecy and Christianity represented divine punishment as physical evil in order to arouse the anaesthetized conscience of the people of God:

> Accordingly, a scourge has an eminently curative function. It is not visited upon humanity to bring about the people's death, but so that the people (or possibly an individual) should be converted and live. Secondarily (and this is where we encounter the major difference from the usual notion of divine punishment), this physical affliction does not necessarily affect the guilty party. It can also hit the innocent, who must then pay for the behaviour of the entire people. The supreme example of this is Christ himself, the sacrificial victim for the sins of the people. In this sense every disease and every affliction is a divine punishment. Sick individuals purify themselves by accepting the burden of suffering and offering it up for their brothers and sisters. Moreover, the people of God share in Christ's sacrifice and supply what is still lacking in his suffering.

Grasping these points helps us to understand that the use of the term "divine punishment" for AIDS excludes any form of disdain or discrimination towards those suffering from this disease. Instead it shows how this scourge can acquire a positive meaning and value both for those who suffer from it and for all other people.[16]

Piegsa reached the conclusion that it was impossible to say Yes or No to the question whether AIDS was a divine punishment. Instead it was bound up with one of the most problematical of human questions – the problem of suffering in the world.[17]

Reference to original sin is a committed acknowledgement that, on the one hand, God is not the cause of suffering and death (and therefore not of AIDS); and that, on the other hand, human beings are guilty, because 'Sin made its entry into the world through one man, and through sin, death' (Rom 5.12). With regard to this reference to original sin, however, Eid pointed out that the *peccatum originalis* certainly had to do with a fundamental sinfulness of human beings, but that this did not absolutely suffice to explain the irrational nature of dire cruelty and of the threats to which humans are subject: 'Terrible suffering and the wicked burdens that weigh fatally upon the human race are and remain irrational.'[18] Even though it is understandable that some people should resort to speculations about AIDS that avoid declaring that individuals are responsible because of their personal behaviour, yet adhere to the doctrine of original sin in asserting that there is a association (although it is impossible to say exactly how it is inherent in the human condition) between suffering (and therefore between AIDS as well) and human guilt, Eid rightly warns us to be 'extremely wary of speculating so simplistically about a problematical topic that is highly complex theologically, and certainly still very far from having been satisfactorily resolved, and to refer accordingly . . . to the assurance of faith that God chooses to be our partner in this condition in which we are so afflicted by pain and suffering. Otherwise, once again, all that confused and deceptive speculation about the how and wherefore of sin and suffering will disqualify and exclude those affected by that sin and suffering.'[19] Speculations about the connections between AIDS and guilt have 'enmeshed disease and those who suffer from it in . . . a whole web of innuendoes about sacrificial victims and expiation that have turned sick people into sacrificial offerings for their own sins, and made sickness a way of expiating sinful behaviour.'[20]

Ideological distortions ensure that one's own disease, which is actually an illness to be cured, is no longer seen as AIDS. Instead the classifiable disorder is viewed as a sexual lapse: as an evil which then replaces AIDS itself as the condition to bewail and escape from: 'Good morals means good medicine.'[21] Statements like this seem attractively logical if one is looking for certainty and trying to bolster it with a superficially rational explanation. But one's own infection by HIV and AIDS, and even one's own responsibility, whatever it may be, are all too quickly obscured. The image of God concealed behind talk of punishment, or citing God as a warning, as conveyed in statements of this kind, is designed to evoke deceptive anxieties with which sex can be associated, just as use was made in the past of the threat of venereal disease or of the fear of having an illegitimate child. Then as now, however, fear does not engender morals. But it does produce a kind of dual morality that results in a superficial change in behaviour – but only as long as the specific danger looms. Fear is always a bad adviser. This is also true of theological ethics, since in general fear is not conducive to an inner confrontation and even to a possible change in behaviour, because moral behaviour depends essentially on freewill: on, that is, freedom of choice and action. Gründel also quite rightly refers as follows to the particular complex of problems associated with arousing anyone's fear of a sexually-related infection: 'What is more, any anxiety-inducing threat is of scarcely any account, especially in matters to do with sex. All it does is to awaken a suspicion that a dire situation is being exploited in order to persuade people to behave correctly. Moral systems, moralists, and church authorities that try to push people to do or not to do certain things by scolding and chastising them come over as elements of a 'moral police force.' Everything should be done to avoid any suspicion that moral theologians and the Church are intentionally using fear to make people behave reasonably – as they see it.'[22]

Contributions by authors who have treated AIDS as a consequence of general moral licentiousness, or as a result of sexual liberation, have often been influenced by the overriding need to assert that traditional sexual standards are right after all, and to demand strict adherence to them. It must be objected to all those who have discussed AIDS exclusively as an ethical topic, or at least primarily in terms of sexual morality, and in so doing have intended a practical instrumentalization of moral requirements such as loyalty, marriage and abstinence, while citing the danger of catching a disease as a reason for the 'right' sexual behaviour, that all they have done is to use this illness as an excuse for sexual moral exhortation and admonition. Even in the first stage of discussion of the subject, Gründel pointed out that the notion of ethics and morality offered by any such restricted moral theological way of looking at sexuality, which had moulded the traditional

Christian understanding of the subject for centuries, was quite inadequate. The purpose of moral theology was no longer confined to the training of confessors. We have to realize that that kind of 'sin morality' was finally dispensed with as outdated with the breakthrough to new theological perspectives that began with Vatican II.[23] But the fact that, after the Council, it is still necessary to point out the potential threat to genuine pastoral work represented by the total exploitation of illness and by a rigorist morality of the sexual life, is shown, for instance, by the following basic advice for anyone exercising a pastoral ministry: 'There is no real difference between seeing that someone is in a desperate state and then projecting your own prejudices onto the situation, and wanting someone to be in a desperate state so that you can preach about it all the more impressively. Love brooks no hypocrisy, we are told in Romans 12.9 ("Let love be without dissimulation"). A kind of grim apologetical relish of human difficulties is not the right way to go about pastoral work.'[24] A third approach is when you are pleased that someone is in a desperate state because you can see an opportunity to let your own prejudices prevail. In fact, some people were 'very happy to represent homosexuals as scapegoats whom they could make entirely responsible for the problem, coupling the accusation with a demand to stop behaving like that, and thus prevent the plague from spreading.'[25]

The representation of aspects of sexual morality as the primary and essential task of Christian ethics in response to the worldwide spread of HIV and AIDS, and to the devastating consequences of the epidemic, must be seen as a degradation of Christian morals to the level of a crude morality in which everything is seen in terms of coital behaviour. Questions of sexual ethics that were suddenly updated, as it were, when the pandemic began – such as extramarital sex, homosexuality, birth control, and artificial insemination – still have to be discussed, but independently of HIV/AIDS. The current estimate of about 39.5 million people worldwide infected by HIV, 95 per cent of whom live in so-called developing countries, means that the challenge for the Churches, too, and for theologians, cannot be a matter of examining topics proper to sexual ethics before anything else, let alone of proposing the Church's moral teaching as the sole response to AIDS.

As yet AIDS remains an incurable disease, but by now the quality of life of those infected with the virus can be maintained for many years by intensive treatment – given a functioning health system that makes this possible. Accordingly, medical successes have rightly demonstrated the untenability of the equation HIV = AIDS = death, which many people had taken for granted initially. Medical knowledge has also helped to banish the assignment of AIDS to the category of myth, and to ensure that it is now viewed primarily as what it is: a life-threatening infectious disease – no more and no less. To that extent, not even the fact that John Paul II's message of 11 February 2005 for International Patients' Day with the keynote 'Christ, the hope of Africa' once again referred to AIDS as a 'patologia dello spirito' (a pathological condition of the soul) is cause for alarm.[26]

In addition to its actual medical meaning, the mention of AIDS also brought to mind terms that conveyed the overall nature of the social climate to a considerable degree at the beginning of the epidemic, and even now to some extent: exclusion, intolerance, discrimination, and complacency. Instead it should remind us of enlightenment, integration, humility, and solidarity – those ongoing achievements that AIDS challenges the international community, individual regimes, the Churches, and theologians, but also every single person, to bring about. We need:

– Enlightenment as the most important weapon in the armoury of those waging a successful war against the global epidemic;
– Integration of those suffering from it, so that they do not experience the fight against AIDS as a crusade against those who are infected and sick from the disease;
– Humility in the sense of an acknowledgement that one's own ideas of morality cannot and are not intended to be shared and lived by everyone;
– Solidarity with the individual but also as commitment to a form of macro-justice that goes beyond distributing condoms and clean needles for drug addicts. It also means provisions to ensure that all people have the opportunity of education, can assert their human rights and equal rights for women, and end the seemingly inescapable round of poverty, malnutrition, and HIV-infections. The international community must rise to this challenge.

Translated by J. G. Cumming

Notes

1. Bernhard Hülsebusch, 'Ehe-Annullierung wegen Aids? These eines Priesters führt zu Streit unter Italiens Katholiken', in: *Stuttgarter Zeitung* (21.3.1996), p. 20.
2. See the extensive treatment by Frank Sanders, *AIDS als Herausforderung für die Theologie. Eine Problematik zwischen Medizin, Moral und Recht*, Essen, 2005 (= *Münsterischer Kommentar zum Codex Iuris Canonici* 43), pp. 167–310.

3. Dietmar Mieth, 'Aids – die ethische Exponiertheit der Probleme', in: Ernst Burkel, *Der AIDS-Komplex. Dimensionen einer Bedrohung*, Frankfurt am Main & Berlin, 1988, pp. 408–24, esp. 408.

4. Beate Jakob, 'Was bedeutet HIV/AIDS für die Kirchen?', in Aktionsbündnis gegen AIDS (ed.), *HIV/AIDS. Ethisch-theologische Fragen und Antwortversuche*, Tübingen: Fachkreis Ethik, Theologie und HIV/AIDS des Aktionsbündnisses gegen AIDS, 2004), pp. 3–4, esp. 4.

5. See, e.g., Rocco B. Buttiglione, 'Ist AIDS eine Strafe Gottes?' in: *Leben: Warum? AIDS* (German edition of: *Dolentium Hominum. Church and Health in the World. Journal of the Pontifical Concil for Pastoral Assistance to Health Care Workers* 5, 1 (1990), being the proceedings of the Fourth International Conference Vatican City, 13–15 Nov. 1989, pp. 159–164, esp. 160.

6. Antonio Autiero, 'Anthropologische und ethische Überlegungen zum Thema AIDS', in: Helmut R. Zielinski (ed.), *Prüfsteine medizinischer Ethik XI*, Grevenbroich, 1988, pp. 52–85, esp. 69.

7. 'Anyone who says that AIDS is a divine punishment is merely telling the world that he or she thinks God is cruel.' Cf. Johannes Gründel, 'Widerspruch zwischen Gesundheitspolitik und ethischen Normen der Kirche?', in: Hanspeter Reinz & Hans Mendl (eds), *AIDS. Eine Herausforderung für die Theologie*, Augsburg, ²1997, pp. 62–73, esp. 67. Furthermore, with regard to the scriptural data, Mieth says that we '. . . must not confuse sickness and guilt. There is no warranty in the New Testament for any connection between sickness and guilt. We have to stop projecting our own fears onto other people.' Cf. Diermar Mieth, *Aids – die ethische Exponiertheit der Probleme*, op. cit. supra., p. 422.

8. Georges Cottier, 'AIDS: Ein Zeichen der Zeit?', in: *Leben: Warum? AIDS: Dolentium Hominum*, op. cit. supra, pp. 34–41, esp. 35.

9. Volker Eid, 'Strafe Gottes und Chance für eine bessere Liebeskultur? AIDS aus der Sicht theologischer Ethik', in: Torsten Kruse & Harald Wagner (eds), *AIDS. Anstösse für Unterricht und Gemeindearbeit*, Munich, 1988, pp. 33–51, esp. 39.

10. As early as 1984, investigative surveys showed that in Kinshasa AIDS infected men and women to the same extent and that there was no association between the victims and homosexuality, drug abuse, or infected blood. It proved possible to trace individual cases of heterosexual transmission back to 1980. Observations of groups of infected haemophiliacs show that up to 10 per cent of female partners were infected, and a study in the *Journal of the American Medical Association* for 15 Mar.1985 reported a 70 per cent rate of transmission of the disease from AIDS patients to their wives. Laun's assertion even in the sixth edition of his book about marriage, love, and partnership seems questionable in this context: 'The most frequent mode of transmission of the terminal infection occurs in homosexual sexual intercourse and as the result of promis-

cuity, and therefore as a consequence of two modes of behaviour that the Church defines as sin.' – Andreas Laun, *Liebe und Partnerschaft aus katholischer Sicht*, Eichstätt, [6]2000, p. 124.

11. Christa Meves, 'Glaubensverlust bewirkt Niedergang – über die innere Logik der Verfallserscheinungen', in: *Theologisches* 24 (1994), 267–74, esp. 274.

12. Hans Kramer, 'Ethische Zwischenbilanz zu Aids', in: *Stimmen der Zeit* 114 (1989), 371–82, esp. 379.

13. Joachim Piegsa, *AIDS. Krankheit und Herausforderung*, Mönchengladbach, 1987, p. 8.

14. 'Every era has its own "menetekel" (cf. Dan 5.25), which it should neither ignore nor suppress. We cannot carry on as if nothing had happened. An extreme erosion of humane values has taken place that penetrated to the very foundations of our culture. Aids ought to be interpreted as an urgent call for reflection', *ibid.*, p. 13.

15. Georges Cottier, 'AIDS: Ein Zeichen der Zeit?', in *op. cit. supra*, p. 41.

16. Rocco Buttiglione, 'Ist AIDS eine Strafe Gottes?', in *op cit. supra*, pp. 163–4.

17. See Joachim Piegsa, *AIDS. Krankheit und Herausforderung*, *op. cit. supra*, pp. 11–3. Statements like this show that Kienzler is correct in identifying a mechanism that comes into operation if the search for a guilty party fails – a shift from anthropodicy to theodicy. Cf. Klaus Kienzler, 'AIDS geht uns alle an. Menschliche und theologische Bemerkungen', in: Hanspeter Heinz & Hans Mendl (eds), *AIDS. Eine Herausforderung für die Theologie, op. cit. supra*, pp. 84–92, esp. 89.

18. Volker Eid, '"Strafe Gottes" und "Chance für eine bessere Liebeskultur"? AIDS aus der Sicht theologischer Ethik', in: *op. cit. supra*, pp. 33–51, esp. 38.

19. *Idem*, 'AIDS: Nur eine Solidaritätskultur hilft', in: *Imprimatur* 21 (1988), 49–51, 51. Accordingly Eid's recommendation is: 'We must remain unflinching in our rejection of the explanation of AIDS as a consequence of guilt or a punishment for sin, and we must do so theologically too, indeed precisely as theologians, and we must not allow this absolute rejection to be called in question by confused talk of a supposedly given association between human sin and the incidence of evil.' – *Idem*, 'Strafe Gottes und Chance für eine bessere Liebeskultur? &c', *op. cit. supra*, p. 41.

20. Marciano Vidal, 'The Christian Ethic: Help or Hindrance?', in *Concilium* 1997/5, pp. 89–98, esp. 96. '[AIDS] is, basically, a disease, and has to be treated as such. All other considerations, concerning its cause or concerned to make value-judgements, are exposed to unwarranted falsifications and extrapolations', *ibid.*, p. 92.

21. John J. O'Connor, 'AIDS: Wissen und Gewissen', in *Dolentium Hominum &c, op. cit. supra*, pp. 16–25, 24.

22. Johannes Gründel, 'AIDS– eine Herausforderung an Christen und Kirchen', in Wolfgang Klietmann, (Ed.), *AIDS. Forschung, Klinik, Praxis, soziokulturelle*

Aspekte, Stuttgart & New York, ²1990, pp. 241–54, esp. 250.

23. *Idem*, 'AIDS – Anlass zur Enttabuisierung ethischer Fragestellungen', in *AIDS. Forschung, Klinik, Praxis, soziokulturelle Aspekte, op. cit.*, p. 85.

24. Hubert Windisch, 'AIDS und die Pastoral', in *Theologie der Gegenwart* 31 (1988), 95–101, esp. 99.

25. Helmut R. Zielinski (ed.), 'Der Seelsorger und die AIDS-Patienten', in *Prüfsteine medizinischer Ethik XI, op. cit. supra*, pp. 105–29, esp. 113.

26. See John Paul II., 'Messagio per la XIII giornata mondiale del malato' (8.9.2004), published online under: http://www.vatican.va/holy_father/john_paul_ii/messages/sick/documents/hf_jp-ii_mes_-20040929_world-day-of-the-sick-2005_it.html (18.10.2006).

Four of the Tasks for Theological Ethics in a Time of HIV/AIDS

JAMES KEENAN

Since HIV/AIDS first appeared more than twenty-five years ago, the pandemic has prompted those in ethics to reflect on how we as a people, whether as health care clinicians, public health officials, theological ethicists, vulnerable constituencies, or simply taxpayers, critically ought to respond to the crisis. Here then, I examine where theological ethicists have taken critical initiatives, the reasons why these initiatives were taken, and the direction ethicists must subsequently pursue.

I. Critically considering the care, cultural context, and actual delivery of healthcare

One of the most fundamental areas of investigation concerns the use of industrialized medicine and technology to respond to the crisis both to prevent transmission and to treat those already infected. While the initiatives are gravely needed, questions regarding the context of the local culture and the humaneness of the care being offered have been repeatedly raised by theological ethicists.

Occasionally, the attempt to respond to the HIV/AIDS crisis looks like an industrialized Western military operation seeking to correct and remedy all that it perceives as wrong in a local setting. The language of 'targeting populations' and 'destroying the virus' capabilities' contribute to this perception. More problematic, however, are the way these operations often overrun existing infrastructures of local health care. In these instances, these activities are considerably inefficient, generate false hopes, and undermine existing local programmes. These problems often arise from a failure to appreciate that healing and health care occur and are determined by local culture.

Four examples highlight how Western technology has overlooked local context in HIV/AIDS treatment: Tanzania's Laurenti Magesa writes of the alienation of witch doctors and other African religion leaders from local prevention and treatment programmes in his native Tanzania; Mark Miller describes how the failures and successes in prevention strategies in western Canada depended on a direct engagement of first nation communities there; James Good recounts the unanticipated problems that faced those seeking to treat nomads in Kenya; and Paul Farmer and David Walton described the naiveté of condom distributors working in Haiti. Many, many other instances abound.[1]

Inevitably, the turn to local culture raises a question regarding the quality and humanity of health care: does technology promote or reduce the humanity of health care delivery?[2] For instance, the hype that accompanies pharmacological capabilities often becomes more fascinating than the predicament in which HIV-infected patients find themselves. In particular, Emmanuel Katongole has raised a ringing critique of the inhumanity of certain policies that singularly rely on drugs and impoverish the overall tenor of health care in Africa.[3] These critical stances highlight how moral theologians must be vigilant to the possibility that the mode of delivery of much-needed drugs could dangerously compromise the value of local values and customs as well as objectify and dehumanize the recipients of care as well as their care givers. In the light of the stigma still so deeply attached to HIV/AIDS, the question of the humanity and the context of healthcare is paramount.[4]

Moreover, theological ethicists need to be vigilant also about the research that more and more pharmaceuticals are conducting in the developing world. In 1997, for instance, an extraordinary debate arose over experiments concerning drug programmes to inhibit transmission from mother to foetus.[5] That debate examined whether there were any grounds for compromising research protocols that normally hold universally. Do dire straits prompt us to suspend standards? If so, who bears the burdens when these standards are compromised? Our vigilance is imperative especially as microbicide investigations get underway.

II. Concepts, language and advocacy regarding prevention and access to treatment

'The public language . . . of AIDS is as important as the science,' wrote the casuist Albert Jonsen.[6] In 1997, Jonathan Mann reflected on this claim and argued that the issue of casting a conceptual framework for ethically and politically analyzing HIV/AIDS was urgent. To make his point, Mann put before public health officials a long recognized but rarely addressed insight: 'it is clear, throughout history and in all societies, that the rich live generally longer and healthier lives than the poor.'[7]

Why then was the issue of poverty so rarely incorporated into the language of public health ethics? Mann provided an analysis:

- 'Public health has lacked *a conceptual framework* for identifying and analyzing the essential societal factors that represent the conditions in which people can be healthy.
- 'Public health lacks *a vocabulary* with which to speak about and identify commonalities among health problems experienced by very different populations.
- 'There is *no consensus* about the nature or direction of societal change that would be necessary to address the societal conditions involved.'

Mann discovered in the language of human rights its integral comprehensiveness and moral urgency. For instance, human rights language could link global campaigns for the right to access available medical treatments with equally effective and local strategic movements to obtain greater equality in political, economic, and social forms of life. He therefore proposed that public health had a desperate need for the conceptual framework of human rights to analyze and effectively respond to the unprecedented nature and magnitude of the HIV/AIDS pandemic.

His work has generated two further claims. First, Paul Farmer looked at the inequity of social institutions and how they embody virulent pathologies of power. Reflecting on the deep connection between poor health and poverty, he saw the root causes of disease as being more connected to economics than to biology. He became particularly aware of the structural issues which made possible violence against women and girls.[8]

From a different perspective, global economist Jeffrey Sachs studied how disease affects social structures; that is, how disease makes people poor. While poverty certainly creates the conditions by which people become at risk for poor health, disease destroys their ability to escape from the very context that made them susceptible to ill health in the first place. 'Disease is not only a tragedy in human lives, disease is disaster for economic development.'[9]

Coming from contrary perspectives, Farmer and Sachs do not contradict one another: rather, they keep us on track to see the deep and interlocking connections between poverty and disease.

Theological ethicists have paralleled these developments by bringing the language of the common good, social justice, solidarity, and the option for the poor into their discourse. In many ways Lisa Sowle Cahill pioneered this shift, by engaging the traditional language of Catholic social justice so as to prompt us to be more attentive to issues of power and distribution of resources.[10] In a word, our conceptual framework helps us to bridge the gap between conceptual analysis and social change: we do this because ethics must be socially effective. All of ethics must, as Aristotle and Aquinas reminded us, end in action.[11] Thus, like public health officials, we realize that we cannot make the claims of what is fair unless we have the linguistic instruments to understand why there are inequities and how they can be levelled.

For this reason, ethicists have been able to examine critically the issue of patenting and access to anti-retroviral medicines. What was once considered a simple issue of intellectual property is now confronted by the claims of the human right to basic urgent life-saving goods.[12]

This attentiveness to social justice and human rights also offers us analytical resources to address the underlying causes for ongoing transmissions and therein lead us to more effective and comprehensive strategies for prevention. Here especially we can investigate better why women are so at risk today and why gender equity is such a needed component to HIV/AIDS prevention. For instance, we need to remember that more than a third of all people living with HIV/AIDS are young people between the ages of fifteen and twenty-four, and almost two-thirds of these are girls. Why are girls and young women bearing the burden of the HIV/AIDS pandemic?[13] The languages of human rights and social justice not only reveal to us that sexism and classicism are causes of HIV/AIDS transmission, they also provide us a framework to investigate the proper ways of bringing such power inequities to an end.

III. Bridging the great divide: an anthropology of responsiveness and an ethics of vulnerability

Assuredly, we need to recognize the very real divide between those who are infected by or at risk to the virus and those who are not. Here, Jon Fuller and I propose that the virus particularly thrives where there is instability, a notion that is much more relevant than the frequently cited concept of 'marginalization.' Instability, not marginalization, is what frightens the rest of the world, and HIV/AIDS breeds specifically where there is social instability, whether that means those who are affected by civil strife, military incursions, or liberation armies in Uganda, Haiti, Sudan, or the Congo; those who are refugees in any part of the world; those in the prisons of Russia; those married to South African or Indian truck drivers who themselves live in very unstable worlds; those in debt-ridden nations on the verge of economic collapse; heads of families forced to migrate for employment, and those at home who await them; those who are drug addicts, whose own apprehension of themselves is itself unstable; those who are forced into sexual activity to support their children, their families, or their school fees; those who are overseas workers and fishermen; those who engage in clandestine homosexual activity in homophobic societies; or those girls and young women who are faithful to their marriages or to other stable sexual relationships but whose husbands or partners put them at risk because of external sexual liaisons. In short, we find persons infected or at risk to the virus not simply among marginalized people, but rather as vulnerable persons precisely because their lives and their social settings lack the stability needed to live safely in a time of HIV/AIDS.

Against this threat of instability, more stable societies and institutions (including Churches) have created protective barriers. As opposed to supporting those public-health preventive strategies which protect HIV-vulnerable individuals, some leaders perceive that the better and more important shields are those that keep risky individuals distanced from 'the general population.' Keeping these parties away from the more stable society is also perceived as protecting social mores and communal orthodoxy from contamination.[14]

This isolationism is often backed by a deep moral judgmentalism, whether explicitly stated or not. Donald Messer, in *Breaking the Conspiracy of Silence: Christian Churches and the Global AIDS Crisis*, argues, for instance, that the Churches prompt their congregations to view those at risk to the virus with righteous suspicion. To make his case, he presents several surveys, among them an informal one taken at a World Council of Churches gathering in Harare, Zimbabwe, in 1998, in which 68 per cent said they believed the pandemic to be a punishment from God.[15] In short, the face of AIDS is rarely perceived as being innocent.

This judgmentalism about AIDS has never been dismantled. Because it insists that those at risk are so by their own choices, their predicament receives little human sympathy. A simple contrast to another grave human tragedy, the recent Indian Ocean tsunami, highlights the impact that moral judgmentalism has in validating the divide between stable and unstable societies.

The number of lives lost to the tsunami approached 300,000. This tragedy generated billions of dollars of supported response within weeks. Although HIV/AIDS causes the same number of deaths every thirty-seven days, the will to commit concomitant resources to prevent such loss of life simply does not exist. Not only that, but if every thirty-seven days another tsunami were to occur, we would witness a global effort of the highest priority creating a wall protecting all of humanity against the threat of such tsunamis. Faced with the fact that the HIV/AIDS pandemic does sustain the loss of 300,000 persons every thirty-seven days, we find no such interest in building a wall against the 'sea' of the virus. Desiring to protect ourselves from those at risk, we build a barrier against those living in unstable worlds.

Theological ethicists respond directly to this reality. Messer's work is a comprehensive, accessible response to the isolating tendencies promoted by our Churches. He tries to call the Churches to a realization of their complicity in the isolating strategies that leave unstable societies even more at risk. In a similar vein, Maria Cimperman seeks to prompt the Churches to respond to the crisis by asking what type of transforming, embodied anthropology we need to articulate for our faith-communities if at present they are so inept and insular.[16]

These attempts to prompt the people of God to take long-awaited initiatives in response to this pandemic serve as foundations for other ethicists to continue the work of alerting their communities from the apathetic slumber that we are presently witnessing, still twenty-five years into this pandemic.

As Cimperman and Messer work on their side of the divide, Enda McDonagh finds himself among those living on the unstable fringe and offers an ethics of vulnerability. Standing with those who are stigmatized, who encounter as the crucified Christ did the harsh reckless judgment of the masses, McDonagh suggests that we need to develop a theology of vulnerability to sustain those at risk, those infected, and their care-givers who live in an unsettling, unstable, and isolated world.[17] It is here, where HIV/AIDS is in-breaking, moreover, that McDonagh discovers and reflects upon the in-breaking of the Kingdom.[18] Like his colleagues on the other side of the divide, McDonagh offers promising foundations for further theological work in guiding those from the community of faith already immersed in the chaos of HIV/AIDS.

IV. Prevention: the condom

Because rates of infection are outdistancing rates of treatment, the issue of
effective prevention strategies is even more urgent today than ever. Among
these, the ABC strategy is considered the most effective programme: First,
A: Abstain; delay onset of intercourse until marriage. If you can't abstain, or
are already in a sexual relationship, then B: Be faithful to that partner. If you
choose (or do not have the freedom to say 'no' to) sexual relations, then C:
use a condom.

How reliable is the condom? We should acknowledge that condoms are
not 100 per cent reliable and that they can break, degrade under improper
storage conditions or with inappropriate (petroleum-based) lubricants, and
be improperly manufactured and improperly used. However, arguments
that condoms provide no protection are obviated by studies involving their
actual use among humans.

The largest analysis of published, peer-reviewed studies looking at the
question of condom effectiveness was produced by the National Institute of
Allergy and Infectious Diseases of the National Institutes of Health, USA,
in July 2001. There it was noted that HIV is a very inefficiently transmitted
infection when compared with other sexually transmitted diseases. For
example, a single exposure to gonorrhea causes infection in 60–80 per cent
of women. In contrast, after a single exposure to HIV, only 0.1–0.2 per cent
of women become infected. The study found that use of condoms reduces
the already low transmission rate of HIV by 85 per cent. If one applied these
data to 10,000 persons being exposed to HIV during sexual intercourse over
a period of one year, in the absence of condoms 670 would become infected,
while that number would be reduced to 90 if condoms were used consistently and correctly. The conclusion is clear: condoms are not perfect, but for
those who choose (or are forced into) sexual contact, significant protection is
afforded by this method.[19]

Faced with the effectiveness of condoms, Monsignor Georges Cottier,
O.P., theologian of the papal household and president of the International
Theological Commission, was asked in an interview with Vatican Radio
whether condom distribution might qualify as a 'lesser of two evils'
approach. He responded: 'This is the question that moralists are asking
themselves, and it is legitimate that they ask it.'[20]

A few moral theologians, notably Kevin Kelly, have argued that any
teaching on the condom inevitably must grapple with the teaching on contraception. Kelly argues that the teaching on birth control is itself the source

of considerable dilemmas for Catholics and that the issue of HIV-prevention helps highlight the need to develop a more responsible birth control teaching.[21]

Others have argued differently, applying casuistic moral principles (lesser-evil, double effect, cooperation) to demonstrate the compatibility of magisterial teaching on birth control with effective HIV/AIDS prevention methods.[22] These highlight that in the case of HIV, the condom is not being used as a contraceptive device, but as a prophylactic against transmitting a deadly disease. They show how traditional principles acknowledge the legitimacy of such a distinction, and defend condoms for HIV/AIDS prevention while upholding – or at least not contesting – the validity of church teaching on contraception.[23] That distinction – between the therapeutic and the contraceptive – is found in *Humanae Vitae*: 'The Church does not consider at all illicit the use of those therapeutic means necessary to cure bodily diseases, even if a foreseeable impediment to procreation should result therefrom – provided such impediment is not directly intended for any motive whatsoever' (paragraph 19).

These theologians have taken the casuistic position simply to acknowledge that bishops could support condom use without opposing *Humanae vitae*. Yet, twenty years later moral theologians and many other Catholics are confounded by their hierarchy who persist in opposing condom usage by invoking the immutability of the birth-control teaching. Catholics are astonished not simply because they are convinced of condom efficacy, but because their bishops seem to value their own teaching over the lives of those at risk: the present crisis is ultimately a threat to life itself, and not just a threat to sexual mores. The issue of protecting life, the heart of HIV/AIDS prevention strategies, does not appear to be at the forefront of their priorities. Thus, Melinda Gates echoed well the sentiments of many Catholics when she stated at the XVI International AIDS Conference: 'In the fight against AIDS, condoms save lives. If you oppose the distribution of condoms, something is more important to you than saving lives.'[24]

Because of continued pressure from ethicists, public health officials, world leaders, and some of their own more enlightened brother bishops, these bishops will inevitably recognize the moral validity of the condom as part of a prevention strategy. As they do, they will need to decide whether to repudiate the birth-control teaching entirely or to take the casuistic road and distance condoms as therapeutic from condoms as contraceptive. In any event, until they do, they undermine their own authority and leave many millions of lives at considerably greater risk than they need to be.[25]

Conclusion

At the first international conference of Catholic Theological Ethics that met in July 2006 in Padua, 400 theological ethicists engaged a variety of topics in applied ethics, and one overwhelmed all the others: HIV/AIDS and access to health care. As ethicists continue to engage bioethics through the lens of social justice and as those working specifically in the area of HIV/AIDS realize, the world of theological ethics dramatically expands.[26]

So often the concerns of theological ethics and moral theologians reflect the landscape of the neighbourhoods in which we live: stabilized, barrier-driven (though often invisible) enclaves. When we engage HIV/AIDS we find ourselves crossing the great divide, entering into the unstable world where HIV/AIDS thrives. Investigate AIDS and we meet homosexuals, prisoners, truck drivers, prostitutes, emigrating workers, people caught in civil strife, drug users, vulnerable young women, refugees, and a host of others. There we encounter humanity at its most vulnerable. It is there, I suggest, that we find our own vocation.

Notes

1. Laurenti Magesa, 'Recognizing the Reality of African Religion in Tanzania,' in James Keenan (ed.), assisted by Lisa Sowle Cahill, Jon Fuller, and Kevin Kelly, *Catholic Ethicists on HIV/AIDS Prevention*, New York: Continuum, 2000, pp. 76–83; Mark Miller, 'Unmaking a Hidden Epidemic among First Nation Communities in Canada,' *ibid.*, pp. 84–91; James Good, 'HIV/AIDS among Desert Nomads in Kenya,' *ibid.*, pp. 91–6; Paul Farmer and David Walton, 'Condoms, Coups, and the Ideology of Prevention: Facing Failure in Rural Haiti,' *ibid.*, pp. 108–19.
2. Sharon R. Kaufman, *And a Time to Die: How American Hospitals Shape the End of Life*, New York: Scribner, 2005; Bertrand Lebouché and Anne Lécu, *Où es-tu quand j'ai mal?*, Paris: Cerf, 2005.
3. Emmanuel Katongole, 'AIDS, Africa, and the "Age of Miraculous Medicine"', Padua.
4. On the issue of stigma see the essays by Linda Hogan, John Mary Waliggo, and Nicholas Harvey in *Catholic Ethicists*.
5. Ronald Bayer, 'The debate over maternal-fetal HIV transmission prevention trials in Africa, Asia, and the Caribbean: Racist exploitation or exploitation of racism?,' *American Journal of Public Health* 88 (1998), pp. 567–70.
6. Albert Jonsen, 'Foreword,' E. Juengst and B. Koenig (ed.), *The Meaning of AIDS*, New York: Praeger, 1989.

7. Jonathan Mann, 'Medicine and Public Health, Ethics and Human Rights,' in *The Hastings Center Report* 27 (1997), pp. 6–13.

8. P. Farmer, M. Connors, and J. Simmons (eds), *Women, Poverty and AIDS: Sex, Drugs and Structural Violence*, Monroe, ME: Common Courage Press, 1996; P. Farmer, *Pathologies of Power: Health, Human Rights and New War on the Poor*, Berkley: University of California Press, 1998; P. Farmer, *Infections and Inequalities: The Modern Plagues*, Berkley: University of California Press, 2002.

9. J. Sachs, 'Winning the Fight against Disease: A New Global Strategy', Keynote Address to the 2003 Fulbright Scholar Conference, 2 Apr. 2003, p. 2: http://www.earth.columbia.edu/about/director/pubs/FulbrightSpeech040 3.pdf#search=%22%22disease%20is%20disaster%20for%20economic% 20development%22%22 (last visited, 10.06.06).

10. Lisa Sowle Cahill, *Theological Bioethics: Participation, Justice, Change*, Washington, D.C.: Georgetown University Press, 2005; Jon Fuller and James Keenan, 'The Language of Human Rights and Social Justice in the Face of HIV/AIDS,' *Budhi: A Journal of Ideas and Culture* 8 (2004), pp 211–33.

11. Jewish bioethicists make similar arguments regarding justice and 'communal solidarity.' See Aaron Mackler, *Introduction to Jewish and Catholic Bioethics*, Washington, D.C.: Georgetown University Press, 2003, pp. 190–211.

12. Lisa Sowle Cahill, 'AIDS, Justice, and the Common Good, *Catholic Ethicists*, 282–93; Edwin Vasquez, *AIDS Treatment in Brazil: Applying a Catholic Understanding of Human Rights and the Common Good to Pharmaceutical Patents Regarding the Urgent Need of Access to Antiretroviral Drugs*, Weston Jesuit School of Theology Doctoral Dissertation, May 2006.

13. Mary Crewe, 'A pep-talk too far: Reflections on the power of AIDS education,' (May 12, 2005) http://www.csa.za.org/filemanager/list/6/ (visited 08.10.06)

14. These claims are developed in Fuller and Keenan, 'Educating in a Time of HIV/AIDS,' in Julian Filochowski and Peter Stanford (eds), *Opening Up: Speaking Out in the Church*, London: Darton Longman & Todd, 2005, pp. 95–113.

15. Donald Messer, *Breaking the Conspiracy of Silence: Christian Churches and the Global AIDS Crisis*, Minneapolis: Fortress Press, 2004, pp. 5–7.

16. Maria Cimperman, *When God's People Have HIV/AIDS*, Maryknoll, NY: Orbis, 2005.

17. Enda McDonagh, *Vulnerable to the Holy*, Dublin: Columba Press, 2004.

18. McDonagh, 'The Reign of God,' *Catholic Ethicists*, pp. 317–23.

19. National Institute of Allergy and Infectious Diseases, National Institutes of Health, Department of Health and Human Services, 'Scientific evidence on condom effectiveness for sexually transmitted disease (STD) prevention', 20 July 2001 (available at http://www.niaid.nih.gov/dmid/stds/condomreport.pdf).

20. Catholic News Service, 'Papal theologian: AIDS-condoms issue legitimate to debate', 15 Feb. 1996.

21. Kevin Kelly, *New Directions in Sexual Ethics: Moral Theology and the Challenge of AIDS,* London: Geoffrey Chapman, 1998.

22. An application of each of the principles is made in Fuller and Keenan, 'Condoms, Catholics and HIV/AIDS Prevention,' *The Furrow* 52 (2001), pp. 459–67.

23. For a review of these theologians works, see *Catholic Ethicists,* pp. 21–9.

24. Melinda Gates, 'Address to the XVI International AIDS Conference, Toronto, 13 Aug. 2006. http://64.233.161.104/search?q=cache:aXAhgbMiDxEJ:www.gatesfoundation.org/MediaCenter/Speeches/MelindaSpeeches/MFG Speech2006AIDS-060813.htm+Gates+%22oppose+the+distribution+of+condoms,+something+is+more%22&hl=en&gl=us&ct=clnk&cd=5 (visited 10.06.06)

25. Fuller and Keenan, 'Church Politics and HIV Prevention: Why is the Condom Question So Significant and So Neuralgic?', in Linda Hogan and Barbara FitzGerald (eds), *Between Poetry and Politics, Essays in Honour of Enda McDonagh,* Dublin, Columba Press, 2003, pp. 158–81.

26. James F. Keenan, 'Developments in Bioethics from the Perspective of HIV/AIDS', 'Cambridge Quarterly of HealthCare Ethics, 14.4 (2005), pp. 416–23.

III. Experiential Approaches

Metaphor, Illness, and Literature, or Lunch with Nikolay Stepanovitch

STEVE DOWDEN

> 'Illness is the nightside of life.'
> – Susan Sontag

How does the metaphorical dimension of literature influence the way we see the world? In everyday, non-literary, speech, metaphors play an obviously significant role. They both reflect and structure the way we perceive the world, how we think, and consequently how we react to certain circumstances. Our responses to the idea of death, for example, or to the idea of disease are expressed in the language we use to talk about them. If we say, for example, 'He lost his battle against AIDS,' we are seeing a man's illness and death in terms of military engagement and defeat. Perhaps such everyday usage is neutral, perhaps not. But in literature, where language is most precisely, most forcefully, and most significantly at work, we might reasonably expect the stakes and rewards to be high. Insofar as literature is more than just an escape from boredom, we ought to expect it to help people see the true world more fully, more clearly, and with deepened understanding. And metaphor, far from being a merely decorative feature, should be a tool in this enterprise of disclosing the truth.

I. Corrupted metaphors: A battle against 'meaning'

Curiously, one of our era's leading literary commentators expresses grave doubts about using metaphor at all in matters of disease and dying. In *Illness as Metaphor* (1978) and its companion piece *AIDS and Its Metaphors* (1989),

Susan Sontag explores the harmful effect that metaphor can exert in our understanding of disease and its effect on us all. The first essay grew out of her own experience as a cancer patient. In her dealings with the disease that eventually killed her, Sontag found that the cultural myths surrounding cancer deepened and worsened its effects. She had not only to see to the healing of her body, which was difficult enough; she also had to face the gloom, isolation, and sense of guilt that the idea of this disease produced in the people she knew and in her own mind.

The idea of cancer – an ensemble of prejudices, fears, and myths – arises because metaphorical 'meaning' attaches to it, a meaning that is itself malignant. Cancer is, so to speak, the invisible enemy within, not the explicable and thus manageable result of some outward cause. Cancer, she suggests, is conventionally viewed as a bodily response to repressed emotion, to passion that is blocked or suppressed. Bottled up inside the body like some evil genie, this powerful force takes on the malign form of a tumour: an uncontrollable inward growth that the sufferer has himself called into being, that is in fact somehow an expression of the self. Consequently the tumour's supposed 'meaning' points toward a life not sufficiently open, one that is cramped, bitter, flawed. Such metaphors, in their turn, draw their strength from our collective fear of an illness whose processes remain largely a mystery, one that can strike any of us without warning – not unlike the afflictions that tested the biblical Job: a good man struck down by invisible forces. In Sontag's view, we must demystify illness by refusing to assume that diseases can 'mean' anything at all. A disease must be seen with a clear eye for what it is and not as a symbol for something else. After all, some dangerous diseases do not readily absorb meanings. Pneumonia is just pneumonia. And even one of the most devastating plagues of the twentieth century, the influenza pandemic of 1918, appears to be untouched by hysterical metaphor.

There are signs that even cancer is shedding its encrustations of meaning. By the time Sontag published *AIDS and Its Metaphors*, a decade after *Illness as Metaphor*, much progress in the study and treatment of cancer had been made. The meanings that shadowed it had by then begun to disappear. However, this effect may partly have to do with the emergence of AIDS as an epidemic, with its special potential for metaphorical construal. In the 1980s, AIDS in Western countries was largely judged – in the strong sense of the word – to be a disease of homosexual men, prostitutes, and drug addicts. With such handy scapegoat groups in easy reach, much pious *Schadenfreude* went into the metaphors of divine wrath and harsh justice: the

Lord punishes the wicked. Now that the worldwide and heterosexual dimensions of the pandemic have become clearer, these primitive and self-serving views appear to be subsiding. Still, other sorts of pernicious metaphor remain in place.

II. Invasions from the South, invasions from the East

For example, there is a long tradition behind the idea that epidemic disease has a military character. Contagious illness 'attacks' the body from without and 'destroys' it from within. An epidemic such as AIDS 'invades' society. Doctors and researchers must 'battle' the disease with all the 'weapons' at the disposal of modern medical science, which has 'declared war' on AIDS.

In addition, we are constantly reminded that AIDS has its origins in Africa. Now, this is no doubt a fact (though Sontag doubts it), but as she persuasively argues, facts are not often allowed simply to rest on their neutral status as information or knowledge. They acquire secondary meanings, usually moral meanings. The Asiatic cholera pandemic of 1826–1837 raged in Europe once it arrived from India. Yet Europe's own cholera – fostered by its unsanitary living conditions – persisted in the European imagination as something alien, something Asian and oriental, which is to say: primitive, irrational, mysterious, and deadly.

In Thomas Mann's *Death in Venice* (1912), cholera is made metaphorically to express the moral corruption of the novella's protagonist, Gustav von Aschenbach. As the great writer gradually gives himself over to the decadent pleasure he takes in spying on a beautiful Polish youth, cholera takes his body. Sweet corruption destroys him morally just as surely as the cholera that has swept into Europe from the East pollutes and destroys his body. Mann informs his readers about the disease in prose that is itself sultry, luxuriant, and decadent:

> For several years now, Asiatic cholera had been showing an increased tendency to spread and migrate. Originating in the sultry masses of the Ganges delta, rising with the mephitic exhalations of that wilderness of rank useless luxuriance, that primitive island jungle shunned by man, where tigers crouch in the bamboo thickets, the pestilence had raged with unusual and prolonged virulence all over northern India; it had struck eastward into China, westward into Afghanistan and Persia, and Astrakhan and even to Moscow.

On the streets of Venice Aschenbach indulges himself in some sweet, soft, overripe strawberries. They poison him with Asiatic cholera and finally, as he gazes longingly at the boy Tadzio on the beach, Aschenbach dies in a secret ecstasy of decadence, enervation, and disgrace. Outwardly his public dignity remains intact, but inwardly he has succumbed to the seduction of beauty and desire. In Mann's novels and stories, the deepest seductive beauty is embodied in Slavic boys and women – Clawdia Chauchat, Tadzio, Pribislav Hippe, Esmeralda – which is to say, a threat that comes from the East.

III. Sickness and sin

The Western idea that forces of disease, disorder, and doom invade from the East is very old. In Greek myth, Dionysus imports chaos and death from the East in Euripides' *The Bacchae*, and the fiendish child-killing Medea is a sorceress from the East as well. Supernatural powers, sexual desire, and epidemic disease – as in *Oedipus Rex* – are linked by the idea of a secret connection between corruption of the body and moral corruption. In modern literature this commingling of geographical and moral categories is nowhere so plain as in Bram Stoker's *Dracula* (1897), a novel and thematics whose enormous popularity in contemporary fiction, music, television, and film is linked to AIDS via its versatile mingling of disease with religion, moral decadence, and sexual morality. This book is a master narrative of epidemic contagion as the metaphoric embodiment of moral pollution.

In Dracula we have a perversely inverted parody of Christ, an immortal capable of bestowing immortality on his disciples. Those whom he converts do not perish but receive an everlasting life. He is of course from the East. Though Dracula's home lies in Europe, Stoker makes clear that his clan is descended from Mongol invaders of the early Middle Ages. The Asiatic blood in his veins, such as it is, must be replenished from that flowing in the bodies of healthy men and women, boys and girls of England. Like the epidemic of sex and blood that he represents (syphilis in Stoker's day, AIDS in our own), the vampire strikes opportunistically and promiscuously. He will take what he can get but seems to prefer debauching young men and women.

In Stoker's novel, the sweet virgin Lucy is the central figure, a submissive and nubile girl in whose body mingle the life fluids of five different men. Her fiancé Arthur gives her his blood and regards the gift as a sacred symbol of wedlock before the fact. He does not know that her two other suitors and

Dr van Helsing have also given her infusions, and they tactfully conceal from him Lucy's metaphorical promiscuity. Finally, though, it is Dracula who carries the day. Or night. Under the influence of his 'kiss' Lucy becomes a lascivious and unmistakably sexual predator. He has awakened the demon within her, so that after her conversion she has become 'a devilish mockery of sweet Lucy's purity,' as one of her horrified suitors puts it. Stoker's novel is transparently a parable about the dangers of feminine sexuality when not held in check by social and religious moral law. Lucy's is a corruption that she spreads like an epidemic, one that is carried in the blood.

A tale such as this, endlessly reiterated and varied in high and popular culture, has obvious potential for guiding our view of AIDS in unwholesome directions. Its very popularity and persistence suggest that it may reflect or even structure the way many people – consciously or subconsciously – perceive the transmission of AIDS, and how we view those who are afflicted with it. Moreover, Stoker's way with the metaphor of disease is not so different from the manner in which Mann links erotic desire with illness. Mann's protagonist is not a simple girl, so easily undone in Stoker's novel, but a great moralist, a mature writer, internationally celebrated for his constancy of moral will and tenacity of purpose. Aschenbach's slide into a corruption that is simultaneously spiritual and somatic carries the same subliminal message as Stoker's narrative: moral corruption and contagious disease are linked at a deep level.

IV. Can we get by without metaphors?

Now, probably almost no one actually subscribes at a conscious level to this notion that disease and moral corruption are conjoined. It is a metaphor, not a concept. However, narrative metaphors may well sink much deeper roots than rational concepts. The fact that these tales are so compelling, have proved so durable, and are so familiar among literary readers suggests that at some deeper level they may in fact have a profound hold on our imaginations and so shape the way we see the world. Still, Susan Sontag's dark view of metaphor and illness sits uneasily. After all, when she writes with beautiful and evocative concision that 'illness is the nightside of life,' she too is relying on metaphor.

Can we really get by without recourse to metaphor, in daily life or in literature? May it not also be the case that metaphor sharpens and illuminates our vision rather than leading it astray? Perhaps a part of the problem here resides in the attitude and expectations we put in literature, especially great literature. In seeking to clarify this problem, I will turn now to two stories that address the way that literature and metaphorical or narrative thinking take hold of living experience or, in this case, the experience of illness and dying: Leo Tolstoy's *The Death of Ivan Ilyich* (1886) and Anton Chekhov's 'A Dreary Story: From the Notebook of an Old Man' (1899). In the age of AIDS, the special claim that these stories have on our serious attention is plain. Each directly explores the meaning of life from the perspective of death. Each focuses attention on a protagonist who is dying of a fatal illness. But each also expresses a fundamentally different view from the other in such a way as to illuminate the problem at hand: the tension between lived experience and the metaphorical dimension of literature.

(a) Tolstoy: a tale of redemption

In *The Death of Ivan Ilyich* Tolstoy imagines a protagonist who has squandered his life in petty ways on material things. He clings pretentiously to his career as a government official, to his unhappy marriage with a grasping social climber, to shallow relationships with his social and professional equals. He has a daughter, Liza, who studies music and is on the cusp of making a very advantageous marriage to a man who, like her father, is a prosperous lawyer.

One day while climbing a ladder (an apt metaphor for his way of life) Ivan suffers a fall (another metaphor, this time biblical: he 'falls' into awareness of the human mortality). Ivan has bruised his left side and at first thinks nothing of the injury. However, the wound does not go away and gradually he falls ill. Over the course of a few months his condition and the pain in his side worsen. The doctors offer much advice, all of it useless. Plainly Ivan is dying. He knows it, and the people around him know it. Yet they treat his illness as an awkward imposition on their social calendars:

> He saw that the awesome, terrifying act of his dying had been degraded by those about him to the level of a chance unpleasantness, a bit of unseemly behavior (they reacted to him as they would to a man who emitted a foul odour upon entering a drawing room); that it had been degraded by that very 'propriety' to which he had devoted his entire life.

Moreover, family and friends insist on upholding the fiction that he will recover – not for his sake but simply out of cowardice, as a way of avoiding the necessity of giving death and illness their due respect:

And he was tortured by this lie, tortured by the fact that they refused to acknowledge what he and everyone else knew, that they wanted to lie about his horrible condition and to force him to become a party to that lie. This lie, a lie perpetrated on the eve of his death, a lie that was bound to degrade the awesome, solemn act of his dying to the level of their social calls, their draperies, and the sturgeon they ate for dinner, was an excruciating torture for Ivan.

Only the household servant – a strong healthy youth named Gerasim – has the grace, goodness of heart, and simple tact to treat Ivan with kindness and human understanding. Such figures are pivotal in Tolstoy's fiction. Civilized, rationalist, Westernized characters such as Ivan have become alienated from the earth, from true human experience, and even from their own souls. The good-hearted peasant serves to recall them, and Tolstoy's readers, to themselves.

In the end, as Ivan's agony worsens, he comes to see that he himself has been living a lie. His whole wasted life 'was not the real thing but a dreadful, enormous deception that shut out both life and death.' However dreadful his illness and pain may be, they are at least 'the real thing', as he puts it, and his dying agonies also afford him one last opportunity for true human experience. While screaming and flailing in the final torment before his death, Ivan's hand falls on his young son's head. Vasya is a boy of perhaps ten, still young and innocent. Like the peasant Gerasim he is not yet corrupted by the shallow ideals of Russia's *haute bourgeosie*. The boy spontaneously, lovingly and with no ulterior motive seizes his father's hand, kisses it, and begins to weep: 'At that very moment Ivan Ilyich fell through and saw a light. . .'. It is a moment of epiphany and transformation. Ivan can now die reconciled. 'It is over,' says a voice in the room – or a voice from John 1.9. Echoing Revelations 21.4, Ivan's final words are, 'Death is over . . . there is no more death.'

In Tolstoy's story there is a good deal of tension between the felt life of the human situation and the metaphorical burden the story is made to bear. By the end of the tale, Ivan Ilyich's story has plainly become a parable of Christian redemption. The teller, Tolstoy, now presents himself as part moral philosopher and part preacher. His tale has a didactic force. Illness is equated with the human condition – our mortality – and death is the night-threat that should compel us to seize the day. But here is the problem: if fiction is a way of knowing the world, how should we think about fiction that lays claim to a truth that lies outside of storytelling itself, a matter of

Christian doctrine for example? Tolstoy uses the power of narrative and metaphor to communicate a specifically Christian message about illness and death.

(b) Chekhov: A tale, and no redemption

Chekhov's approach in 'A Dreary Story' tells a similar situation with a crucial difference at the end. At a time when he was himself suffering from a fatal illness – he died of tuberculosis in 1904 – Chekhov imagines a man facing death, perhaps even in direct response to *The Death of Ivan Ilyich*. His protagonist, not unlike Ivan Ilyich, is prosperous, respected, and accomplished. Nikolay Stepanovitch is an elderly professor of medical research and a privy councillour who moves in the foremost intellectual and social circles. He enjoys worldwide prestige for his scientific work and has revelled in the triumphs of his life. But now, he can no long sleep at night. He takes no more pleasure in his beloved lectures, which have also fallen off in quality. He feels unwell. Like Ivan, Nikolay Stepanovitch has a pampered, self-absorbed daughter who studies music (a frivolous luxury in this context), and he has a wife from whom he has grown apart. Unlike Ivan, he is able to diagnose his own failing health. Nikolay Stepanovitch knows that he has fewer than six months to live. And like Ivan, this illness awakens him, brings him into a more reflective state of mind.

Still he must see to his responsibilities, though. The great professor is accustomed to people relying on him for guidance. When a young physician comes to him seeking a topic for a doctoral dissertation, Nikolay Stepanovitch flies into a rage, haranguing the poor supplicant. He does not, he cries contemptuously, dispense research topics like some shopkeeper who keeps them in stock on a shelf. The whole point of independent scientific research is that it be *independent*. He relents, however, and dismisses the man with a humdrum topic. For better or worse, this is how the world works. Still, Chekhov's point has been made: true science is a matter of independent thought, not fame, patronage, or even the fatherly guidance from some acknowledged authority. Knowledge is a matter of considering the evidence with an unprejudiced eye, not of following some prefabricated script, doctrine, or canon.

Likewise, literature – taken seriously as a way of knowing the world – is a matter of independent thinking, an adherence not to preconceived canons of thought, belief, or art (or the established metaphors that represent them) but to a fresh, unprejudiced encounter with the particularity of living experience. In the case of this story, the living experience that Chekhov seeks imaginatively to explore is the experience of dying.

Nikolay Stepanovich also has within his circle a young woman whose life experience has been tragically out of the ordinary for his class. Katya was his ward as a child. As she grew up she conceived a passion for the theatre, fell in love with a scoundrel playwright, gave birth to an illegitimate child that died in infancy, and now lives near her guardian's home as a public scandal. In terms of narrative structure, she would appear to play a role like that of Tolstoy's peasant-sage Gerasim, or the unspoiled child Vasya: an outsider figure whose function it is to bring the protagonist to his senses and put him in touch with deep human values. It is to her that Nikolay Stepanovich repairs when his vapid family life and the fear of death become too much for him: 'I fly to you, I beg for help.'

Lonely and languishing in self-pity, Katya has no help to give. Rather, in her misery and despair she wants him – the wise professor of medicine, the expert on sickness and health, on life and death, her legal guardian after all – Katya wants Nikolay Stepanovich to tell *her* what *she* must do with *her* life. However, the great doctor is not fooled by his fame. He has no moral wisdom to dispense (which knowledge is itself a piece of moral wisdom) and is too honest to pretend otherwise. Katya continues to demand counsel from him, and at the end of the story this exchange occurs:

> 'Help me!' she sobs, clutching at my hand and kissing it. 'You are my father you know, my only friend! You are clever, educated; you have lived so long; you have been a teacher! Tell me what am I to do!' [. . .]
>
> A silence follows. Katya straightens her hair, puts on her hat, then crumples up the letters and stuffs them in her bag – and all this deliberately, in silence. Her face, her bosom, and her gloves are wet with tears, but her expression now is cold and forbidding. . . . I look at her, and feel ashamed that I am happier than she. The absence of what my philosophic colleagues call a general idea I have detected in myself only just before death, in the decline of my days, while the soul of this poor girl has known and will know no refuge all her life, all her life!
>
> 'Let us have lunch, Katya,' I say.

Katya remains furious at him for his refusal to tell the secret of a happy life – or a happy death. There can be no such formula, as he well knows. Instead he tries to return her from intellectual abstraction to the world. Chekhov's wonderfully understated 'Let us have lunch' is a bracing counterpoint to the grand pathos of Ivan Ilyich's deathbed conversion. The living, present moment and his genuine affection for his niece are contained in his appeal to her to join him for a meal – not least of all because we know, as he does, that he does not have many such midday meals left to him. There is gentle and ironic comedy in the invitation, of course, but it is a kind and human comedy.

As death approaches, Nikolai Stepanovitch experiences no great epiphany of the meaning of life. Unlike Tolstoy, Chekhov scrupulously sticks to lineaments of experience. Here we find ourselves in the neighbour-hood of the second commandment. The making of false images is not only a matter of counterfeit gods; it also has an earthly perhaps aesthetic meaning: 'Thou shalt not make thee any graven image, or any likeness of any thing that is in heaven above, or that is in the earth beneath, or that is in the waters beneath the earth' (Deut. 5:8). Chekhov refuses to set down as fixed literary image any piece of moral experience or wisdom that might harden into a 'general idea,' a graven image of sorts. As an artist and a scientist, Chekhov was a respecter of particularity and individuality, of the mobile fluidity of human experience and its evanescence. To embalm such a moment in a metaphor is to falsify it. He did not want to be understood as a shopkeeper dispensing prepackaged doses of religion, moral philosophy, or scientific doctrine.

V. Let us have lunch

Consequently, as a writer, Chekhov was exceptionally cautious with his metaphors, which – as Sontag points out – have a way of taking on lives of their own, of becoming 'general ideas.' The sheer unexpected freshness of his 'Let-us-have-lunch' moment in 'A Dreary Story' cannot be resolved into the same kind of programmatic meanings that Tolstoy's *Death of Ivan Ilyich* insists on. Our understanding of illness and death require of us powerful and clear expression, and this expression will have to be metaphorical – in the age of AIDS or any other. But as both Sontag and, especially, Chekhov warn, metaphors must not be allowed to fossilize into graven images.

The Memory Book

CAROL LINDSAY SMITH

What is the Memory Book? It's a framework to help parents or carers to write or record family history and traditions, personal information and important contacts for children who are at risk of losing touch with their birth family and community. Whether the parents have died or they have been separated through war, migration, or family breakdown, young children quickly lose their sense of identity. The Memory Book can help to preserve some of the knowledge and feelings that would otherwise be lost for ever. The ideas are easy to understand, so, for parents who would find it difficult to write, or who are too ill to cope with paperwork, the whole process can be handled verbally with a helper asking trigger questions and tape recording or writing down the information. What matters is to capture the personal details, the emotions, hopes, and fears which parents would normally share with their children over the years.

The first Memory Books were developed in 1991. As a social worker for Barnardos's, I set up Barnardo's Positive Options in 1991. This London-based agency helped families with HIV/AIDS to make plans for the future care of their children. Many of these parents were from Africa, cut off from family and friends. They did not expect to survive to see their children through to independence and their overwhelming fear was what would happen when they died, leaving the children isolated from the extended family, with no clear idea of their origins and traditions. I started to urge these parents to write down essential information for their children, but it was difficult for them to know where to start. They needed a structure, and so, with their help, we wrote guidelines which became the Memory Book. Later on the book was followed by the Memory Store – a beautiful box with tiny drawers to store mementoes, photos, tapes, anything that would help children recall the ordinary daily life of their family. (Later, to fit the African context, the Memory Store became the Memory Basket or the Memory Tin Box.)

Since this small start Memory Book ideas have travelled round the world, turning up in different forms to fit in with local needs and cultures.

Although they were originally designed for parents with HIV/Aids, the ideas have been easy to adapt to help families facing loss and separation for many other reasons including divorce, imprisonment, and death from other causes. It seems that, however desperate the circumstances, making a Memory Book (or box, basket, tape, video . . .) seems to repay the emotional and practical effort – therapeutic for the writer and uniquely beneficial for the recipient.

Impact of making Memory Books. Parents and carers from very different cultures found the ideas easy to understand and adaptable to their own family circumstances. For many of the African families the idea of writing about the family background was a natural continuation of the oral tradition whereby, in more settled times, children gradually absorbed the history, culture, beliefs, and rules of their community through story telling and listening to adults talk. They were enthusiastic about writing the family history and welcomed the 'space' to write about themselves as real people in healthier times, not just to be remembered as a dying parent. But perhaps most valuable to the parents was the idea that they could also leave a legacy of parental guidance and hopes for the future of their children.

A wonderful outcome of writing their books was that many parents began to ask themselves, 'Why am I not talking to my children about this?' The children themselves were curious about their parents' 'homework', and in some cases the children were needed as scribes for parents who could not write or who were too ill to write. Thus it was a natural transition from writing to talking directly with their children about very personal issues. In situations where children would soon be orphaned or separated, it was then only a short step to involve them directly in making plans for their future care. For families who managed this communications breakthrough it brought enormous benefits to both parents and children in terms of mutual understanding, trust, emotional preparedness for the future, and in some cases a less devastating outcome when the parent died.

Needless to say, there were also parents who found it too harrowing to talk to their children because they could not see any way forward. In such cases, even if they wrote a few lines, set aside a few mementoes, not all was lost.

Nothing new under the sun. The idea for Memory Books grew out of the experience of Life Story Book work, a method of re-constructing the history of children who were marooned in the child-care system and who needed to understand their past in order to move on to a more settled future. When the massive scale of HIV infection amongst families became clear, with the inevitable result of huge numbers of children who would suffer multiple losses, it seemed worth up-ending the Life Story Book methods of reconstructing a lost history, to make it as easy as possible for sick and traumatized parents to tell the family story themselves before it was too late

The Memory Book arrives in Africa. In 1995/6 the Memory Book was shown to Beatrice Were, who was then co-ordinator of NACWOLA[1] in Uganda. Beatrice and NACWOLA members, all of them mothers living with HIV/Aids, quickly realized these ideas could give them a lead into talking frankly to their children – the first step towards making plans for the future. Over the next few years many parents created beautiful, emotional, and also highly practical records for their children. Many of them reported that once the lid was off the family secret, relationships with their children improved dramatically and energy could now be put into constructive planning for the future. Many of these pioneers went public and the ideas spread across Uganda and beyond.

Memory Book for Africa. In 2000, with the help of eight mothers who had already made books for their children, the original Memory Book text was rewritten to make it more user-friendly and culturally appropriate in African countries. The women were frank and forceful about some of the controversial information they believed should be passed on.

Every member of this editorial group had endured discrimination, poverty, and isolation as a result of their HIV status. Property-grabbing after the death of their husbands and being violently punished for bringing HIV into the marriage, regardless of evidence to the contrary, were routine. Several of the women also disclosed having endured tribal or cultural practices they now knew were dangerous. Although they might not live to protect their children, they hoped their words would strengthen resolve to break with tradition – and not to suffer in the same way. For these reasons they worked hard to build opportunities into the text that would give other parents a place to advise and protect their children, particularly girls, from the humiliation and exposure to risk they had faced themselves.

The Memory Project training programme. With support from Save the Children Fund and further input from the original team from the UK, the Memory Book and related ideas were built into a series of workshops with the aim of giving parents the confidence and know-how to alter the dynamics of their family's life and, in some instances, break with tradition or cultural norms.

It is difficult now to recall our state of ignorance, prejudice, and fears about AIDS in the early 1990s. In Uganda and elsewhere in Africa support services for parents and children scarcely existed. It was difficult and dangerous for affected women to disclose their status or take any steps to prepare their children for the precarious future. In many families children could see for themselves that parents were dying, but the wall of secrecy made it impossible to ask questions about the future. In too many cases children would not know how or where they would live after the funeral and there were (and still are) many sad cases of brothers and sisters being shared out amongst relatives at the graveside, with nothing tangible to help them remember the past or reunite in the future. In other cases children were warned not to leave their home to attend the funeral for fear that relatives would grab their property.

The training programme that grew out of memory work with grassroots women therefore tried to give parents the tools to knock down the wall of silence inside their homes, so that they could start to talk and listen to their children and work out strategies with them about how to survive in the future. Most of the training content was new territory for women in Uganda at that time and for many of the participants this would be their first experience of formal training. Topics included:

- The basics of child development and how children of different ages can be helped to anticipate and survive separation and loss;
- Practical experience of how to start talking to children about previously taboo subjects – sexuality, relationships, HIV transmission, illness, death;
- The importance of expressing feelings, *listening* to children, helping them build up a realistic understanding of the family background, beliefs and responsibilities; allowing them to ask questions and taking their views into account;
- Making Memory Books, baskets, and boxes, wherever possible involving children in the process;
- Bringing children into discussions on plans for their own future, finding reliable support systems and appointing guardians;
- Financial and legal information, helping parents to understand the importance of registering property and will-making and how to do it.

Over time parallel training courses were put on for children and for community members who needed better understanding of how they could support sick parents and orphan children in future years.

What is described above is the ideal, and different components of the training programme have taken place as and when funding and trainers have been available. But the attrition of illness or death of leaders, poverty, hostility to dissemination of anti-traditional ideas, even in-fighting among groups who wanted to claim the ideas for their exclusive use, mean that training is patchy – and never enough.

Dissemination. The intention was always that parents who had first-hand experience of HIV, and who had metamorphosed into advocates of open communications and forward planning, would become the next generation of trainers. There were many examples of young women with little or no previous education who jumped the rapids in this way. There were also touching instances of participants putting the new ideas into action overnight – like the mother who came back next day to say 'last night I *listened* to my child.' Despite very limited resources and reliance on amateur trainers, these ideas have nevertheless moved across Uganda and to many other countries in Africa and beyond.

Ten years on the Memory Book and the training programme have been copied, borrowed, and adapted by numerous community-based organizations as well as most of the big NGOs who work with HIV/AIDS. The originators of the materials are thankful to see the ideas filtering down to the vast audience of families and children who need them, especially when there is so little else in the way of psycho-social support for the growing army of orphans and other vulnerable children. It would be all the better if more of them could remember to acknowledge Beatrice Were and the other courageous mothers who were involved in the early days of developing the ideas and who took the risk of sharing their private information in a very public way.

Is the Memory Book and training parents to plan for their children still relevant now that anti-retroviral treatments are capable of prolonging life for people with HIV? Unfortunately there is no end in sight to the rise in new infections and many millions of people already infected have little or no chance of being salvaged by hi-tech medicine when they don't even have the basics of life – clean water, regular food supplies, proximity to a clinic. For these families, and the multi-millions of children who will be prematurely orphaned, we can only hope that a few of the ideas on open communication in the family may filter down and provide some comfort in the years ahead. At least ideas are free.[2]

The future. The team who put the Memory Book together and helped to develop the training programme are setting up a website which will provide free and easy access to all the original materials. It will include:

– the Memory Book text in English and other languages as they become available (currently Luganda and KiSwahili are ready to go);
– the full training programme with background information, exercises and handouts;
– support information for new trainers;
– links to other sources of relevant information;
– details of training programmes and support groups in different countries;
– and more. . . .

The website will be available mid-2007 on www.memory-book.info

Notes
1. The National Community of Women Living with HIV/AIDS (NACWOLA) was set up in Uganda in 1995 by Beatrice Were and a small group of other HIV+ women who decided to disclose their status, fight stigma, and help each other live positively. In 1996 Carol Lindsay Smith showed the Memory Book to Beatrice and her colleagues. They quickly realised that it could help them with their hardest challenge – talking openly to their children about HIV in the family.
2. The Memory Book for Africa is published by Teaching Aids at Low Cost (TALC), PO Box 49, St. Albans, Herts AL1 5TX, or contact via talc@talcuk.org.

IV. Global Justice and AIDS

AIDS, Global Justice, and Catholic Social Ethics

LISA SOWLE CAHILL

This essay will look at the global AIDS crisis through the lens of Catholic social teaching; it will also examine Catholic social teaching in the light of AIDS. Catholic teaching, founded on the dignity of the person, the common good, and care for the poor, offers a solid base on which to defend the rights of all those suffering from AIDS. The interdependence of the person and the common good offers plenty of grounds to attack poverty, lack of access to medical care, oppression of women, multiple sexual partners, and intravenous drug use, all of which are primary causes of the spread of HIV/AIDS. On the other side, however, the global AIDS crisis presents challenges to Catholic social ethics. It must be reconceived to provide a response to AIDS and AIDS policy that is truly global and effective, and that empowers affected persons and communities.

Specifically, the threat and reality of AIDS show that: (1) Catholic teaching about sex and gender must be integrated with Catholic social ethics, so that the criterion of justice is applied consistently; (2) calls for justice, solidarity, and participation must empower decision-making for and by those who suffer injustices; (3) theories about the common good must engender practical social action; (4) the 'common good' framework must move beyond its focus on national governments to include both local and transnational agencies and networks; and (5) the terminology of Catholic social teaching must become more ecumenical and flexible.

I. Global AIDS: some facts[1]

The AIDS pandemic has already caused over 25 million deaths, and almost another 40 million are currently living with HIV/AIDS, including 2.3 million children. Of these people, 95 per cent live in low- and middle-income countries, and most of those infected with HIV are unaware of their status. The peoples of sub-Saharan Africa have been hardest hit by AIDS, with rapidly rising rates in the Caribbean. Adult prevalence in Haiti comes second only to African countries. Moreover, there is increasing concern about the spread of the disease in Eastern Europe and Asia, with a 'next wave' of infections predicted for Russia, China, and India. Over 15 million children have already been orphaned by AIDS.

Girls and young women are the most rapidly growing AIDS population; in sub-Saharan Africa, three young women are being infected for every young man. Gender inequities in socio-economic status and in access to prevention and care subject women to disproportionate risk, as does sexual violence. In addition, women bear much of the collateral burden of AIDS. Women care for sick family members, assume more responsibility for orphaned children, may be cast out of families or communities or lose property if they are widowed or infected, and may even be subjected to violence if their HIV status is discovered.

HIV/AIDS has an impact on virtually every sector of national and cultural life. Economic development and food security are impeded when the working-age population is cut off; deaths of adults in their prime undermine education by removing teachers. Illness and lack of family income and nutrition erode school enrollment and attendance. Demand for health services rises in inverse proportion to loss of skilled professionals, putting unbearable strains on the public health infrastructure of developing countries. By 2010, life expectancies in several highly-affected countries could drop to below forty years, reversing gains of the last century.

Global devastation wrought by AIDS has evoked attention from the international community. The United Nations has called for joint commitment to end the crisis. International initiatives include The United Nations General Assembly Special Session on HIV/AIDS and 2001 Declaration of Commitment on HIV/AIDS; the Global Fund to Fight AIDS, Tuberculosis and Malaria (headquartered in Geneva under the WHO); the World Health Organization's '3x5' Initiative (to provide AIDS drugs to three million people by 2005); and the United States' 'President's Emergency Plan for AIDS Relief' (PEPFAR). Global funding is on the increase. Most aid comes from international donors, primarily the G8 Countries and the European Commission, through bilateral programmes and contributions to the Global Fund. Nevertheless, national governments and local efforts of civil society in affected regions play increasing roles in the response.

The U.S. is the largest single donor, channelling most of its donations through a federally-run programme, rather than co-operating in donations to the multinational, public-private Global Fund. In 2003, President George W. Bush pledged a $15 billion, five-year, aid initiative, stipulating that one third of prevention spending is to be dedicated to abstinence and fidelity education (rather than condoms). $200 million was designated for faith- and community-based organizations. In 2006, US federal funding against AIDS in developing countries was expected to total $3.2 billion, including funds for prevention, care, treatment, and research, as well as $545 million donated to the Global Fund. International spending on HIV/AIDS has risen overall from $300 million in 1996 to almost $9 billion in 2006 (projected as of this writing). Yet resources available still fall far short of need. UNAIDS estimated that $15 billion would be needed to meet the requirements of effective response in 2006, and that the need would rise to $22 billion by 2008.

Lack of resources has, of course, affected the ability of countries to promote prevention and to provide life-prolonging care for those afflicted, and to enable the ability of families and communities to survive, remain intact, and function well. Prevention programmes reach only about one in five of those in need, and only about 20 per cent of people with HIV/AIDS in low- and middle-income countries have access to antiretroviral therapy. In this regard it is important to note recent developments in patent control over AIDS-related pharmaceuticals. According to international trade agreements, companies can 'segment' the market for their products, charging different prices for the same product in different countries. In 1998, worldwide attention was called to the fact that drug pricing aimed at 'first world' markets, as well as patent protection prohibiting local manufacture of generics for developing world populations, was preventing millions from access to life-saving medicines.[2]

In 1998 the government of South Africa passed a law permitting the importation of cheaper drugs, in violation of rules governing patents set up by the World Trade Organization's Agreement on Trade Related Aspects of Intellectual Property (TRIPS). South Africa had over four million people affected with AIDS. The normal cost of the triple-drug 'AIDS cocktail' in the West was $10,000 to $15,000 a year. The companies that hold the patents had agreed to charge about $1000 a year per patient in Africa, still far beyond what countries on that continent could afford.

A lawsuit against the national government by a South African consortium of transnational pharmaceutical companies resulted in the mobilization of local AIDS activists and international AIDS networks, NGOs, UN officials, competitive generics manufacturers, and other diverse media voices. These included Medecins sans Frontières, Oxfam, the European Union, the World Health Organization, and the National AIDS Council of France, as well as high-level representatives of mainline Christian denominations, including the Catholic Church. In June 2001, the United Nations endorsed a 'Declaration of Commitment on HIV-AIDS' and established the world-wide $7–10 billion Global Fund to prevent and treat AIDS and other diseases.[3]

In the end, trade restrictions were relaxed, beginning at the 2001 meeting of the World Trade Organization in Doha, Qatar. Countries experiencing an AIDS health emergency are now able to manufacture or import much cheaper antiretroviral drugs, though resistance from 'first world' countries and corporations continues. Although many countries remain unable to afford even the lowered prices or to effectively deliver drugs to the neediest even when drugs are available, others, such as Brazil, Thailand, and Uganda have been success stories.

On a positive note, the estimates of adult HIV/AIDS infection were lowered in many countries from 2003–2005. Changes in sexual behaviour are partly responsible for these decreases, though mortality of those affected may play a part. According to UNAIDS Executive Director Peter Piot, young people in Uganda, Kenya, and Zimbabwe are having sexual inter-course at later ages, have fewer sexual partners, and use condoms more. He attributes these improvements to global AIDS funding, more open discus-sion of the realities of AIDS, and enhanced community-based programmes. Yet he maintains that African countries need to assume more financial responsibility for AIDS treatment, if treatment is to become sustainable.[4] By December 2005, 18 developing countries had met their '3x5' target, and the number of persons receiving ART had increased from 400,000 in 2003 to 1.3 million. Still, only one fifth of persons in need of treatment in developing countries were receiving it in 2005, and fewer than one in ten pregnant HIV-positive women received therapies that could prevent transmission to the child.

II. Resources of Catholic Social Teaching

The twin foundations of Catholic social teaching are the dignity of the person and the common good. Beginning with the first papal social encyclical, Leo XIII's *Rerum novarum* (1891), these two premises have grounded the Church's efforts to call attention to the plight of the poor in different eras and cultures and to rally efforts on their behalf. The Second Vatican Council reaffirmed that all persons are made in the image of God, and are entitled to share in the common good, which includes 'the entire human family' and 'everything necessary for leading a life truly human' (*Gaudium et spes*, nos 24–6). Since the mid-twentieth century, the common good has been recognized to mean the universal common good, for which there is an international political and economic responsibility, often tied to international government as embodied by the United Nations (Paul VI, *Populorum progressio*, nos 76–8).

Solidarity is central to the thought of Paul VI, and John Paul II repeatedly emphasizes this social virtue. Solidarity is the necessary antidote to structural sin. Rich nations and classes should curb market capitalism and adopt greater concern for international justice. Solidarity 'is not a feeling of vague compassion or shallow distress at the misfortunes of so many people, both near and far. On the contrary, it is a firm and persevering determination to commit oneself to the common good. . . .' (John Paul II, *Sollicitudo rei socialis*, no. 37). Although John Paul II's focus is the responsibilities of the governments of nation-states, he does recognize that local communities, especially those suffering oppression, have a right to 'present their own needs and rights in the face of the inefficiency or corruption of the public authorities' (*Sollicitudo*, no. 39). Moreover, John Paul II decried violence against women, including sex-trafficking and rape, and asserted that women have rights to equal respect and a share of the common good equal to men (see *Familiaris Consortio*, nos 22–4). In a 'Letter to Women' written for the 1995 Beijing U.N. Conference on Women, he condemned crimes against women, lamenting that 'women's dignity has often been unacknowledged and their prerogatives misrepresented; they have often been relegated to the margins of society and even reduced to servitude' (no. 3).

Finally, John Paul II appreciated that the common good includes health care and protection from risk of disease. He applies this specifically to AIDS, saying 'care and relief centres for AIDS patients' can 'give everyone new reasons for hope and practical possibilities for life' (*Evangelium vitae*, no. 88.) Before most people realized the magnitude of AIDS as an international crisis, John Paul II asserted: 'AIDS threatens not just some nations or societies but the whole of humanity. It knows no frontiers of geography, race, or age or social condition. The threat is so great, indifference on the part of public authorities, condemnatory or discriminatory practices toward those affected by the virus or self-interested rivalries in the search for a medical answer, should be considered forms of collaboration in this terrible evil which has come upon humanity.'[5]

In 2004, the pope urged, 'Humanity cannot close its eyes in the face of so appalling a tragedy,' and a Vatican representative excoriated international pharmaceutical companies that keep the price of necessary drugs out of reach of the poor.[6]

As recently as November 2006, an international group of Catholics and Jews met in South Africa to discuss AIDS, led by Cardinal Walter Kasper and Rabbi David Rosen, Chief Rabbi of Israel. They reaffirmed the image of God in all persons. Despite differences on 'possible prevention strategies', the group agreed on 'education, treatment, care, especially for the orphans and people affected by AIDS, and the need to eliminate stigmatization and marginalization'. They urged responsibility to 'all those suffering, threatened, and victimized by this tragic pandemic. This call goes out especially to governments and all who have the power, means, and influence to implement it.'[7] Clearly, then, Catholic social teaching provides abundant resources to attack the AIDS crisis, and to favour protection of the poor, especially women and children, with an aggressive ethic of intervention and justice. Yet the Catholic Church is not generally perceived as an outstanding supporter of those AIDS endangers, much less as a leader in creating just global AIDS policies.

III. Renegotiating the Catholic Response to HIV/AIDS

While a Catholic ethics of human dignity and the common good speaks eloquently to the AIDS crisis, this crisis also reveals the tradition's flaws.

(1) The tradition teaches universal dignity and equality and advocates a preferential option for those excluded from access to material and social goods. However, this teaching is not applied consistently to those suffering from AIDS. The Catholic Church advocates strongly for affected children, but not for those judged responsible for their disease (homosexuals, non-monogamous heterosexuals, and IV drug users). As far as women are concerned, even innocent victims of disease receive a tepid response. Commitment to universal dignity is undermined by politicization of the

response to AIDS around other issues, especially women's sexual equality, homosexuality, and condoms.

(2) The 'official' Church calls leaders and governments to serve AIDS victims but invests little energy in empowering victims to mobilize. The result is that proposed and excluded remedies reflect the ecclesial and political agendas of those in control of the status quo, rather than the needs of the victims.

(3) Recommended solutions are measured in terms of consistency with official teaching about sex but are not tested for feasibility and effectiveness, nor accompanied by concrete plans for implementation. Individuals are accused of sin, but global structures of sin are not called equally to accountability. As a result, the Church's response does not connect with the situations of real people, and does little to change real conditions. Victims will not truly be served until the powerful change their own destructive patterns of behaviour.

(4) A significant dimension of AIDS is that it is a global crisis, going beyond the responsibility of individual agents to include transnational entities like pharmaceutical companies, the WTO, international NGO's, international donors, and the U.N. The common good tradition can no longer be limited to the framework of the nation-state, or even to the U.N. as a form of co-operation among national governments. It must confront global structural sin and call for a global response. The universal common good depends on both local and transnational actors, working in co-operation, but not necessarily under the supervision of one global governing body.

(5) To address the AIDS pandemic, Catholic social teaching needs to co-operate with partners from other traditions and cultures. Not all African cultures assume the modern western separation of religion and politics. The vocabulary of common good, human rights, and subsidiarity is useful in Europe and North America, where separation of Church and State is a longstanding principle of public discourse. In some other contexts, this vocabulary is not as powerful as biblical imagery, or appeals to traditional religions and customs.

Revisions of Catholic social teaching are already occurring where Catholic actors and agencies work in concrete programmes to alleviate HIV/AIDS. The most important lesson is that AIDS is a global issue requiring a religious, theological, ecclesial, and ethical response that is not as much 'top down' as 'bottom up'. Catholic themes of subsidiarity and participation are important here. Every person and community has a right and duty to participate in the common good, helping to define what common good means. The principle of subsidiarity refers to reciprocity between smaller and larger social collectives and sources of authority. Originally, subsidiarity was used by Pius XI to define the autonomy that local communities or entities should have from state governments (*Quadragesimo anno*, no. 79). Later, John XXIII turned the principle around to uphold the duty of governments to intervene 'for the benefit of all citizens' (*Mater et magistra*, nos 52–3). Concerning AIDS, national governments and global and transnational bodies have a responsibility to work for the common welfare. However, it is equally important that local communities have a voice, defining their own solutions and demanding change. Local, mid-level, and global agencies and actors need to co-operate to alleviate socio-economic and cultural conditions that increase vulnerability to infection.

An excellent document from the Catholic Agency for Overseas Development of England and Wales (CAFOD) lays out these challenges in a concrete way.[8] CAFOD has over two decades' experience in community-based HIV/AIDS programmes around the world. A key point is that focus on 'prevention' or 'treatment' is inadequate unless it considers all the social factors that put individuals and communities at risk. Too often, faith-based initiatives move from a basic commitment to help the poor and oppressed to specific demands for 'behaviour change' (abstaining from risky behaviours). They fail to recognize that behaviour often is influenced by circumstances over which people have little control. Blocks to genuine change in behaviour and circumstances must be removed. Total and immediate compliance with a proposed ideal of behaviour may be impossible.

The CAFOD report takes a careful look at the 'ABC' prevention strategy developed in Uganda. This three-pronged strategy, 'Abstain-Be faithful-use Condoms', has been touted by some for its effectiveness but disdained by others for a perceived simplistic reliance on abstinence. CAFOD contends that all three prongs are interdependent and must be interpreted in a nuanced, sensitive way. In fact, evidence from UNAIDS and other sources shows that reduction in numbers of sexual partners has been a more effective anti-AIDS strategy than use of condoms alone, since condoms frequently are not used consistently and correctly.[9] Abstinence has multiple meanings: delaying the age of sexual intercourse, or confining sex to a stable relationship, a long-term relationship, or marriage.[10] Similarly, faithfulness can mean marriage, serial monogamy, or simply reducing the instances of casual sex or numbers of sexual partners. CAFOD rejects both flawed programmes of 'abstinence only' and equally dogmatic campaigns rejecting all references to abstinence as too moralistic. All three parts of the ABC program are necessary and complementary. Only under supportive conditions do individuals have genuine options.

ABC applies to governments and public leaders, and even to faith communities, as a social obligation: Advocate for change, Break the silence, and Challenge discrimination and injustice. CAFOD offers Uganda as a case study. From the mid-1980s to the mid-1990s Uganda made great progress in reducing infection rates and securing therapies. Among the key factors were openness about the epidemic, reducing stigma; investment of funds and resources; rapid voluntary testing and counselling; care and support services; 'development of locally led, community-based, culturally acceptable and "home grown" responses using local expertise and with minimal influence from Western/Northern donors, policy makers or advisers'; cultural changes regarding widowhood and property rights; establishment of a Uganda AIDS Commission; peace and employment after fifteen years of war; and economic opportunity, education, and greater legal protection for women.[11]

Let me end with an illustration. In January 2005, I had the opportunity to travel with a U.S. Christian international children's and family aid agency, Holt International Children's Services. We observed the work of a Ugandan Christian agency to which Holt donates funds, Action for Children (AFC).[12] Founded in 1995 by Mrs Jolly Nyeko, AFC is staffed entirely by Ugandans – 39 employees and 45 community volunteers. Operating in seven districts of Uganda, AFC served over 10,000 children in 6,000 families in its first decade, on a budget of only $150,000. AFC's current international aid includes a USAID grant for 'abstinence education'. But the work of this women-led agency goes far beyond advice to 'Just say no'. Its primary focus is support for women (and a few men) who are raising children, grandchildren, and other orphans in villages devastated by AIDS. AFC assists families to identify needs and formulate plans to improve their situations. In part with micro-grants, they produce small vegetable crops for the neighbourhood market, raise goats, chickens, and rabbits, and gradually obtain food and school funds for all children in their care. AFC's goal for each is 'self-sufficiency' in community, enabled by networks of cooperating families and villages supported by Action social workers and trained volunteers. AFC also works with young people in AIDS villages and in camps for refugees ('internally displaced persons') fleeing the violence of the Lord's Resistance Army. Some former child soldiers or soldiers' 'wives' rebuild lives through brick-making; raising chicks in dried-mud, coal-burning incubators; or making clothes and crafts with simple tools and sewing machines.

The focus of AFC is not refraining from sex acts but building a meaningful life in which women have dignity and self-reliance, and in which sex can be integrated constructively and responsibly. Hope for the future saves teens and young adults from the need to trade sex for money or to use sex as a substitute for security, and the temptation to express desperation and rage through sexual violence. The approach to AIDS represented by AFC is local, women-focused, supported by international partners who do not control policy or programmes, and oriented toward the most vulnerable populations. It represents the African values of community, family, and local sustainability. It interfaces with global resources and policies, as well as transnational manifestations of 'civil society', to renew village and family life and strengthen the dignity of persons.

A global Christian ethic for AIDS must respect the dignity and empower the agency of real and potential victims; move decisively from ideals to action; involve local, regional, national, international, transnational, and global actors; and speak the language of multiple audiences, whether common good, human rights, option for the poor, image of God, or other locally potent symbols of dignity and unity.

Notes

1. 'HIV/AIDS Policy Fact Sheet: The Global AIDS Pandemic,' Henry J. Kaiser Family Foundation (Menlo Park CA, May 2006) accessed at www.kff.org, 05.11.2006. See also 'International Assistance for HIV/AIDS in the Developing World: Taking Stock of the G8, Other Donor Governments and the European Commission,' Kaiser Family Foundation, accessed at www.kff.org, 05.01.2005; *UNAIDS 2006 Report on the Global AIDS Epidemic*, May 2006, accessed at data.unaids.org/pub/GlobalReport/2006/2006_GR-ExecutiveSummary_en.pdf, 07.11.2006; and 'The Global HIV/AIDS Pandemic, 2006,' United States Centers for Disease Control, August 2006, accessed at www.cdc.gov, 05.11.2006.
2. For more extensive accounts, see David Barnard, 'In the High Court of South Africa, Case No. 4138/98: the Global Politics of Access to Low-Cost AIDS Drugs in Poor Countries,' *Kennedy Institute of Ethics Journal* 12 (2002), pp. 159–74; and Lisa Sowle Cahill, 'Biotech and Justice: Catching Up with the Real World Order,' *Hastings Center Report* 33 (2003), pp. 34–44.
3. 'From the U.N.'s Statement on AIDS: "Prevention Must be the Mainstay"', *New York Times*, 29 June, 2001, A8.
4. 'UNAIDS Pilot Says Young Africans Are Abstaining From Sex For Longer,

Reducing Number Of Partners, Increasing Condom Use,' *Medical News Today*, 11 May 2006, accessed at www.medicalnewstoday.com/medicalnews.php?newsid=43136, 05.11.2006.

5. John Paul II, Tanzania, 1990, as cited in 'Live and Let Live,' the statement of CAFOD (Catholic Agency for Overseas Development, part of Caritas Internationalis) for the World AIDS Campaign 2003–4, accessed at www.cafod.org.uk/policy_and_analysis/policy_papers/hivaids/.

6. 'Vatican Condemns Aids Drug Firms,' BBC News, 29 Jan. 2004, accessed at http://news.bbc.co.uk/2/hi/europe/3442217.stm, 08.11.2006.

7. International Catholic-Jewish Liaison Committee 19th Meeting, 'Joint Declaration,' Cape Town, South Africa, 4–7 November 2006, accessed at www.bc.edu/research/cjl/meta-elements/texts/cjrelations/resources/documents/interreligious/ILC_joint_communique_06.htm, 09.11.2006.

8. Ann M. Smith, Jo Maher, Jim Simmons, Monica Dolan (London: CAFOD), 'An Understanding of HIV Prevention from the Perspective of a Faith-Based Development Agency,' paper developed from a presentation at the International AIDS Conference, Bangkok, July 2004, accessed at www.cafod.org.uk, 08.11.2006.

9. Ibid., 10.

10. Ibid., 8.

11. Ibid., 12.

12. See the Action for Children website, www.actionforchildren.or.ug/index.html, accessed 05.11.2006.

Escaping the Gender Trap:
Unravelling Patriarchy in a Time of AIDS

GILLIAN PATERSON

'Today, the face of AIDS is the face of a young woman'
Kofi Annan 2002

I. The gender trap

It is a quarter of a century since AIDS came out of the shadows, classified initially as a disease of homosexual men (Gay Related Immunodeficiency Disease, or GRID). Today, worldwide, the commonest route of transmission is heterosexual. In 2005, women made up almost 50 per cent of HIV+ adults, and in sub-Saharan Africa the figure was over 60 per cent. Very young women are particularly affected: in sub-Saharan Africa and the Caribbean, a woman between the ages of fifteen and twenty-four is 2.5 times more likely to have HIV than her male equivalent. Even in countries where HIV is fuelled by injecting drug use, more women are becoming infected: for example in the Russian Federation the proportion of women among new diagnoses has risen by over 50 per cent since 2001.[1] In Swaziland, a recent antenatal survey of pregnant women aged between twenty-five and twenty-nine revealed an HIV prevalence rate of 56.3 per cent . Here in the UK, the number of women diagnosed as HIV positive has doubled since 2000, while the number of babies born to HIV-infected mothers has quadrupled.[2] Given the billions of dollars spent on AIDS research, it is an international scandal that it has taken so long to develop women-controlled methods of protection such as microbicide gels and pre-exposure prophylactic medications.

On one level, this is because women are *biologically* more vulnerable to the virus. The likelihood of a woman being infected through a single act of unprotected sex is double that of a man: more if other sexually transmitted infections are present. But women are also more vulnerable *socially* than men. They often have little or no control over where, when, how, and with whom they have genital sex. Disease-related stigma is more virulent in relation to women, so they get more blame than men, even if they caught the virus from unfaithful husbands. They are more likely be condemned by the Church and to meet with violence or abuse or eviction from the family home, and they are less likely to have anyone to look after them if they are sick. It is on women that the burden falls of caring for others with HIV-related illness and for children orphaned by AIDS. They may be victims of local customs that stop them from inheriting property, even when their property rights are protected by national laws. In some parts of the world normative, religiously-approved cultural rituals involve sexual violence against women, especially widows and young girls.

Sub-Saharan Africa is currently the epicentre of the epidemic. 'It is impossible to traverse the continent of Africa,' says UN special envoy Stephen Lewis, 'without an enveloping sense of horror and despair about the carnage among women.' The terrifying HIV prevalence among young women is 'a stark reminder of the meaning of gender inequality', giving rise to 'a deluge of orphans'. Thus the story of AIDS represents 'an omnibus catalogue of women's vulnerability: rape and sexual violence, including marital rape and domestic violence.'[3] What Lewis does not say is that it also represents an 'omnibus catalogue' of low self-esteem among men. Recent studies have shown that rape, gang rape, or risk-taking behaviour generally are more common in contexts that are lacking in social cohesion, or when men themselves are impoverished, humiliated, demeaned, or oppressed: this is one of the reasons why the social heritage of imperialism, and of apartheid in South Africa, has created such fertile territory for the epidemic.[4]

HIV will not be brought under control until women are better equipped to influence the terms of sexual encounters. Speaking at a conference in Pretoria in 1998, Nigerian theologian Teresa Okure created shock waves in her audience when she claimed that there are two viruses more deadly than AIDS. The first is the one that stigmatizes and demeans women in society, causing men to abuse women and ensuring that being a married woman is, in many African countries, the condition that carries the highest risk of HIV infection. For a woman living in a patriarchal relationship, with little influence over what happens to her body, this 'virus' can be fatal.

But reducing *women's* vulnerability will not in itself be enough, because it is ultimately the behaviour of *men* that drives the epidemic. Men are more likely to inject drugs or get drunk. Men, traditionally, control economic power, and sexual relationships are generally conducted on their terms.[5] But male and female sexuality both connect to deeply-rooted, culturally-embedded understandings of identity, and to what it means to be a 'real man' or 'real woman' in a particular context. Institutions that share this context will generally reflect those understandings – a fact that may be especially true of religious institutions, whose role, anthropologically, is to ritualize cultural constructions of gender and give them supernatural or divine status.[6] There are two ways through this: either (i) deep-rooted social and institutional change or (ii) programmes targeted at changing male attitudes and behaviour. Neither of these seems likely to happen, at least within the time-span of current prevention targets, or until a lot more people have died. And that, in a nutshell, is 'the gender trap' that is highlighted by AIDS.

II. A deadly blessing

The AIDS epidemic, says Kevin Kelly, is a lens that has forced us into awareness of 'certain evils that have permeated human life over the centuries and to which as Church we seem to have accommodated ourselves down the ages. Somehow the AIDS pandemic is exposing these evils in their true colours and their horror and destructiveness is becoming clear, *if only we have eyes to see*'.[7]

In 2002, African church leaders meeting in Nairobi issued a statement admitting that Churches 'have – however unwittingly – contributed both actively and passively to the spread of the virus,' and committing themselves to 'challenge the traditional gender roles and power relations within our churches and church institutions which have contributed to the disempowerment of women, and consequently to the spread of HIV/AIDS'. They would 'address gender roles and relations in families that contribute to the vulnerability of women and girls to HIV infection', and they would 'support organizations that help young women to negotiate safer sexual relationships'[8].

This, clearly, is easier said than done. The stranglehold of patriarchy is such that it permeates the liturgical, pastoral, and teaching life of our Churches, especially the Catholic Church, with its all-male priesthood and its hierarchical structure consisting of celibate men living – for the most part – in male communities. But Catholics are not alone. Christians cannot remain blind to the institutional sexism, homophobia, and patriarchy that have characterised the history of all our Churches. Today these are human rights issues (although religions often claim exemption from contemporary human rights principles); and they constitute an impairment of the full humanity not just of women but of the Church, its hierarchies, and its members. In the context of AIDS, they are undermining the capacity of the Churches to 'choose life' and to create conditions in which their members can do so.

Unwilling to face their own need for structural transformation, church leaders may rather confine themselves to blaming society and calling for change there. In his *Letter to Women*, John Paul II hoped (he said) that the greater involvement of women in society would 'force systems to be redesigned in a way which favours the processes of humanization'[9]. As Tina Beattie remarks, it is unfortunate that this vision seems not, so far, to 'extend to the public life and institutions of the Vatican'.[10]

Western patriarchy is, if anything, exacerbated in the Churches of Asia, Africa, and Latin America, where the traditional 'mission' Churches have often felt it their duty to critique or change the local cultures they found there. As the Chinese theologian Kwok Pui-Lan says, 'Many missionaries, both male and female, accused indigenous traditions of being oppressive to women without the slightest recognition of the sexist ideology of Christianity.'[11] Or as Mercy Oduyoye puts it: 'The sexist elements of Western culture have simply fuelled the cultural sexism of traditional African society. Christian theology has certainly contributed to this. African men, at home with androcentrism and the patriarchal order of the biblical cultures, have felt their views confirmed by Christianity. The Christian churches have not encouraged or even accommodated women who have raised their voices in protest.'[12]

Why are these voices so inaudible? Maybe it is because, at some stage in the conversation about gender you have to speak (or at least *think*) of sex. And that is a problem that has arisen time and again in my own research. In colonial languages such as English, French, or Spanish, sex-talk can be constructed in the language of medicine (too clinical for church); the language of passion (too intimate, too unnervingly emotional); or the language of the marketplace, the bar, or the playground (too coarse). Some local languages do not have words for sexual organs or for sexual activities at all. 'It is so important that people here should be realistic about sex,' says a Kenyan priest; 'but I just don't know what words to use about these things, especially in church.'[13]

Our problems do not end there. For Luce Irigaray, objective speech about *anything* is compromised, because the cultural and epistemological systems through which we articulate our experience are relativized by having been set up in relation to the male subject. Our language itself, she says, is phallocentric, projecting a symbolism that 'enshrines male potency while silencing the feminine'.[14] For Julia Benjamin, the very concept of the individual is the concept of the male subject. If the very language we speak is part of the male love affair with himself, where does that leave the differentiation implied by the erotic?[15]

Christians struggling with these issues, in a time of AIDS, may take some comfort from the thought that they are engaged in a debate that is a cutting-edge one for our time. It is uphill work, though. Let us, for example, take the prevention strategy commonly known as ABC (abstention, being faithful, and condom-use). Emerging from the (currently dominant) bio-medical discourse, it is a classic example of a mantra that claims to be universal but is structured, in reality, around the autonomous, adult Western male. *Abstaining?* For women in much of the world, abstention is not an option. Marriage is a cultural necessity, and so are children; early marriage is common and often much desired; women are economically dependent on their husbands; women do not, in general, control the circumstances in which they have sex. *Being faithful?* Many women are indeed faithful: they are infected with HIV by unfaithful or drug-injecting partners. *Condom use?* What woman or child has ever persuaded a reluctant man to use a condom?

The Ghanaian theologian Mercy Oduyoye is co-founder of the influential Circle of Concerned African Women Theologians. Yes, language is a problem, she says, but it's not just a matter of language, and it's certainly not just a matter of condoms. It is the way we relate to each other that creates the conditions for transmission. 'We are actively *welcoming* AIDS when a person's identity is defined in terms of how successful an adjunct she or he is to the wishes of family and culture. We're actively *welcoming* AIDS by having a culture where young people can't say no to older people, where poverty exists and where women are taught they can't say no.'[16] In a time of AIDS, this is a public health issue, as well as a moral and human rights issue. For women, in a time of AIDS, it may be a deadly blessing that the Church bestows.

III. Choosing to know

In recent decades, many Churches have made strides in addressing structural, liturgical, and pastoral gender bias. When Christians resist such change, it is often because they believe their theology authorizes patriarchal gender-assumptions, the 'deadly blessing' going unchallenged because it is supported by sincerely-held assumptions about the nature of God and of the

Church. A further problem is that many Christians (including many Catholics) *do*, today, recognize the patriarchal character of the Church's iconography and the damage it does. But we don't know what to do about it and we don't want to turn our church life into a battleground, so we simply file this knowledge away in the 'too difficult' box in our heads and go on as before. It is within this warped and dismal gender architecture that we must find the space to move beyond the denial that has so insidiously facilitated the progress of AIDS.

Pressure 'not to know' comes from all quarters, including from women, and it is partly understandable. Patriarchy is not all bad for women. Indeed for many, claims Tina Beattie: 'Patriarchy offers a more benign and protective form of social organization than the free market economy. It has established roles for both sexes, with a distribution of rights and responsibilities that is often more effective and fair than feminism recognizes.'[17]

Further, cultures and institutions do change, but not overnight. This is no time for simplistic or ideologically naïve solutions. If we decide the problems of the dispossessed can only be solved by totally 'dismantling' patriarchy (or capitalism, or carbon emissions, or whatever it may be) then we might as well give up, because these things will not be achieved within the foreseeable future. At a time when gender bias is killing people, what is needed, it seems to me, is the intelligent targeting of theological strategies that are used to justify patriarchy. Among these are certain seriously distorting interpretations placed on the figures of Eve and Mary; the patriarchal and imperialist assumptions of much biblical interpretation; and the lack of an appropriate language for articulating resistance to patriarchy.

First, the iconography of Eve.[18] In common interpretations of the Fall, Eve is the temptress. Men are drawn to her, but men fear her, too, for she – Woman – is the source of human sin, and specifically of sexual sin. This interpretation has had a profoundly negative influence on Christian attitudes to sexuality, and in particular to women, making Eve responsible for God's ongoing anger against humanity. And yet God's attitude to Adam and Eve, in Genesis 3, is more sorrow than anger. Exile from Eden is not punishment: it is just that for human beings, once they have the knowledge of good and evil, Eden – sadly – *cannot* be theirs. Eve, says Beattie, symbolizes 'the experience of alienation that necessarily accompanies the acquisition of knowledge', forcing the theologian to 'leave the paradise of unquestioning intimacy and union with God, in order to pursue the question of God through the alien wilderness of culture and learning'.[19] It is a painful and difficult business facing up to the gender bias of our Churches.

But *choosing knowledge* is the heritage of Eve. It is part of choosing to be human. We *have to* know about AIDS; we *cannot* continue in denial of the gender bias that kills.

But that is not the end of the story. In Christian tradition, fallen Eve is redeemed in virtuous Mary. In Beattie's interpretation, the Mother of Christ becomes the 'New Eve': Eve renewed, renewed in Mary, and able at last to turn her knowledge to the service of life rather than death. And if that is true, then both women and men are called to give up huddling in the gender trap, clutching the security blanket of *not knowing*, and to walk together towards the truth.

IV. Claiming the Bible

In 2001, the Botswanan biblical scholar Musa Dube took four years out from her academic job to become regional theological consultant to the World Council of Churches' Ecumenical HIV and AIDS Initiative in Africa. 'I did not immediately see the connection between my work as a New Testament lecturer and the fight against the disease,' says Dube. Then, one day, she was teaching the synoptic gospels to a class of around 200 students, men and women, most of them between eighteen and forty years old. The infection rate in Botswana was then around 38 per cent among sexually active people. Suddenly, she was struck by 'the fact that almost half my class members might not be alive in ten years time.'[20] On the heels of that thought came another: that this life and death situation was *never addressed in the context of mainstream theological studies.*

In her earlier work, Dube had addressed the complicated challenges of opening up the Bible as a salvific text for African and other colonized women. The urgency of this task came home to her in her work on AIDS. The key question for feminist biblical studies is Elisabeth Schüssler Fiorenza's: 'How can feminist biblical interpretation situate its readings of the Bible in such a way that they do not reinscribe the patriarchal discourse of subordination and obedience?'[21] In Africa and other developing countries, another layer is added to this question (one that affects men as well as women) namely: 'How can post-colonialist biblical interpretation move beyond the imperialist discourse of oppression?' Escape from the gender trap, in a time of AIDS, involves answering both questions in a way that draws on local wisdom and acknowledges the social and religious significance of voices that have formerly been suppressed. However, few clergy or lay leaders were remotely equipped to work at this interface. This called for a major rethink of the theological curriculum itself; new method-ological approaches to Christian formation at the level of the local Church; and also, for Dube as a university-based academic, an end to the days of 'bombing out into the Church then retreating to the safe space of the academy'.[22] Ultimately this formed the basis of the influential network of seminaries and departments of education who are developing ways of inte-grating questions raised by HIV and AIDS into the theological curriculum in Africa.

Carrying out such a programme inevitably involves urging people to face what is *actually* going on rather than what they *would like to think* is going on. Resistance to knowledge can be bitter, she says, and women can get very angry when they are confronted with their own gender-powerlessness. In relation to men, she quotes Tinyiko Maluleke: Men have responded (a) by saying, in various ways, 'our women are not like that, so it must be "foreign influences" that are causing them to speak and act in that manner', and (b) by fleeing from dialogue with women by suggesting that, since they are not women, they will not comment on anything to do with gender.[23]

But HIV will not be contained unless people face its realities. As Dube argues, 'Any theologian, lecturer, leader or worker who . . . wants to con-tribute positively to the fight against HIV/AIDS . . . must not only seek to understand how gender is socially and culturally constructed, how it dis-empowers half of humanity, how it fuels the spread of HIV/AIDS, but also to change gender construction so that it empowers men and women.[24]

V. Finding a voice

For women, says Denise Ackermann, the urgent priority is to break the silence that shrouds South Africa's high-risk sexual culture. AIDS has turned South Africa into a context which, like John Chrysostom's Antioch, is 'grazed thin by death'.

In *Tamar's Cry*, she uses the story of Tamar in 2 Samuel 13.1–22 as a hermeneutic lens for a gendered commentary on the HIV epidemic in South Africa. Tamar is *all* women, *everywhere*, who are abused because they are perceived only as an adjunct to men. About to be raped by her half-brother (therefore ruined), Tamar cries out that 'such a thing is not done in Israel!' Her cry is ignored, because this is a patriarchal system where women's cries of distress are unheard and non-normative.[25]

Ackermann argues our need, in the contemporary world, of a language of lament. Tamar puts ashes on her head, rends her robe, and goes away weeping. She is alone, abused, and discarded: the plight of countless women and children through the ages. However, Tamar's 'such things are not done in Israel' is also a cry of resistance, of her non-acceptance of the situation in which such things are, in practice, done.

For the psalmists, it was the through the language of lament that they were able to articulate their questions about evil in the world. Lament comes 'out of the depths', so it can enable us to develop our capacity for grappling with suffering and evil, both our own and within the structures of society. Once articulated, lament can take on a structured form, colonizing 'spaces that are contained by liturgical boundaries and rhythms' and becoming, in the process, a form of individual and communal mourning, where the pain of *knowing* can be articulated, along with the paralyzing intractability of the gender trap.

Conclusion

This essay has described the 'gender trap' that is undermining AIDS prevention strategies, and in which both women and men are caught. We hear Tamar crying out: 'Such a thing should not be done in Israel', and yet things that should not be done are being done. When Churches collude with the patriarchal practices and assumptions from which the trap is built, they are reinforcing it. In a time of AIDS, the strategies we adopt for *not knowing* about the gender bias of our Churches are a denial of truth and a choice of death over life. 'Choosing death' should not be done, in the Church or in communities that call themselves Christian. Recognition of one's own collusion in this communal *not knowing*, when it is combined with a continuing love for one's Church, is a painful and alienating experience – a true cause for lament, because the trap seems so tightly constructed, the evil so irresolvable. It is also the road to redemption.

Notes

1. UNAIDS AIDS Epidemic Updates 2004 and 2005.
2. UK Public Health Laboratory Service figures.
3. Stephen Lewis in a press interview following a visit to Southern Africa, March 2006   http://www.un.org/apps/news/story.asp?NewsID=17847&Cr=hiv& Cr1=aids.
4. T. Barnett and A. Whiteside, *AIDS in the Twenty-first Century: Disease and Globalisation*, New York: Palgrave Macmillan, 2002.
5. Results of the Panos AIDS and Men research appear in M. Foreman, *AIDS and*

Men: Taking Risks or Taking Responsibility?, London: Panos Institute & Zed Books, 1999.

6. Some religious institutions are, of course, reactions *against* prevailing gender mores.
7. K. Kelly, *New Dimensions in Sexual Ethics: Moral Theology and the Challenge of AIDS*, London: Geoffrey Chapman, 1998, pp. 12–13.
8. *Plan of Action: An Ecumenical Response to HIV and AIDS in Africa,* Geneva: WCC, 2002.
9. John Paul II, 'A Letter to Women', *The Tablet*, 5 July 1995, p. 918.
10. T. Beattie, *Woman*, London: Continuum, 2003, p. 42.
11. P.-L. Kwok, in U. King, (ed.), *Feminist Theology from the Third World: A Reader*, London: Geoffrey Chapman, 1994, p. 68.
12. M. Oduyoye, *Daughters of Anowa: African Women and Patriarchy*, Maryknoll, NY: Orbis, 1995, p. 183.
13. G. Paterson, *AIDS and the African Churches*, London: Christian Aid, 2001, p. 13.
14. L. Irigaray, *The Ethics of Sexual Difference*, tr. C. Burke and G. C. Gill, Ithaca: Cornell University Press, 1993. p. 13.
15. J. Benjamin, *The Bonds of Love*, New York and Toronto: Random House, 1988.
16. M. Oduyoye, Address to University of LaVerne Community, October 2005.
17. Beattie, *Woman*, pp. 60–61.
18. This is intended as a reflection on popular attitudes, not a scholarly analysis of the meaning of Eve and Mary in Christian tradition.
19. Beattie, *Woman*, pp. 74–6.
20. M. Dube (ed.), *HIV/AIDS and the Curriculum*, Geneva: WCC, 2003, pp. 12–13.
21. E. Schüssler Fiorenza, *But She Said: Feminist Practices of Biblical Interpretation*, Boston: Beacon Press, 1992, pp. 5–6.
22. M. Dube, 'HIV- and AIDS-related stigma: Implications for theological education, research, communication and community', in UNAIDS (ed.), *A Report of a Theological Workshop Focusing on HIV and AIDS related Stigma*, Geneva: UNAIDS, 2005, p. 57.
23. T. Maluleke, 'African Ruths, Ruthless Africas', in M. Dube (ed.), *Other Ways of Reading: African Women and the Bible*, Atlanta: SBL and Geneva: WCC, 2001, p. 238.
24. Dube, *HIV/AIDS and the Curriculum*, p. 95.
25. D. Ackermann, *Tamar's Cry: Re-reading an Ancient Text in the Midst of an HIV/AIDS Pandemic*, Stellenbosch: EFSA, revised edition London: Catholic Institute of International Relations, 2002, p. 21.

HIV/AIDS: A Commentary

REGINA AMMICHT-QUINN AND HILLE HAKER

I.

She'd waited to tell Jamal. He was only four when she'd gotten the news.
. . . He was seven . . . when Zoe decided she couldn't wait any longer. She
fixed him a sandwich, sat at the table with him. . . .
—Jamal, honey. You know what AIDS is, right?
   Jamal chewed his sandwich. He held the bread with both hands, like a
child younger than seven. He needed a haircut. Loose corkscrews of
shaggy black hair fell over his forehead and the back of his neck. She
found herself staring at his eyelashes, wondering, would he like a bicycle
for Christmas? Would he be safe on it? He nodded. . . .
—Well, I have it. It got into my blood, and I might get sick. I'll probably
get sick.
—When?
—I don't know. It could happen anytime. I thought I should tell you now.
. . .
—Will you die?, he asked.
—I don't know. I hope not. But I could. . . .
—I don't have it. Do I?
—No, I had you tested years ago, you probably don't remember. The
doctor took some blood, you screamed for half an hour. But no, you're fine.
—Can I go up to Ernesto's?
   He got up and walked to the door.
   (Michael Cunningham, *Flesh and Blood* [New York, 1995], pp. 313f).

—Aida will have so many responsibilities if I'm not here. I'll try to live as
long as I can for her sake.
—Does she know?
Christine looked at me anxiously.
—Of course she does.

—What did you tell her?
—What I had to. She'll have to be a mother to her brothers and sisters when I'm gone, and if my parents are still alive then, she'll be their new daughter.
—How did she take it?
—She was very down, of course.
　　(Henning Mankell, *Ich sterbe, aber die Erinnerung lebt* [Munich, 2006], p. 30).

The concept of 'childhood' is in a state of flux all over the world.

Nowadays, in the rich countries of the northern hemisphere, the protective area of 'childhood' is both established as a commercial realm and in jeopardy as a resource for media exploitation.

In the most impoverished countries of the southern hemisphere children are affected by the AIDS disaster in many ways. They are the HIV-infected babies whose mothers had no access to drugs; they are the HIV-infected infants who were and remain exposed to sexual abuse; they are the children who have to suffer their parents' death; and they are the children who are not allowed to be children because they are the ones who must bear the brunt of the international community's failure to act appropriately.

AIDS rips things apart. It destroys not only those who are infected but the family structures that depend on a sequence of generations. At present, in many countries especially affected by HIV/AIDS, grandparents are bringing up their grandchildren, brothers and sisters are caring for their siblings, and uncles and aunts are looking after their nephews and nieces. Half-orphans and orphans are uprooted by the pandemic. Not only is their financial and social situation precarious, but they are cut off from the social structures proper to specific ages and the sequence of generations. Childhood is gradually becoming a time spent in caring for others and for assuming responsibility. While still children, children are taking over the function of parents, and grandparents must stand in for their children.

In recent years an awareness that it will be impossible to see one's own children grow up and to care for them has made 'memory albums' so important. They show that it is matter of prime concern to continue a family tradition, to leave behind accessible ancestral narratives for those whom AIDS has made members of a generation catapulted into the present, and to maintain a specific history.

What are the implications of the erosion of social and generational family structures for future societies? We still have very few studies of the psychological and social effects of such a process; the only thing we can be sure of is that those who have to deal with the sickness, death, and orphaned state of family members often have to bear the burden of excessive responsibilities. Telling their story provides parents especially with a form of communication that will carry their history and feelings and bond with their children into the future. These efforts represent not only an attempt to ensure that individuals or families are remembered, but an attempt by maintaining a family bond to make the anticipated loneliness and isolation of those who survive one's own death more tolerable.

2.

I asked a question of everyone I talked to in Uganda. I asked them where they thought the illness had come from. The answers were very different.

A startlingly large number of them believed it might really be a disease that the western world was secretly spreading on the continent in order to reduce the number of poor people. From this viewpoint, the virus would be a sophisticated means of mass murder. . . . They were convinced that the death-dealing sickness overwhelming them had been planned in full awareness of its effects. For them the entire western world consisted of a vast army of witches or medicine men intent on genocide.

There were also some people who saw a religious dimension to the fate overtaking them. . . . They suffered noticeably from a degree of self-devaluation that increased their suffering twofold. . . .

Everyone seemed to agree that the calamity had hit the African continent with extreme severity.

Christine said: 'It's as if it could never be satisfied. Everything that I read about this continent seems to show that we Africans spend all our time and effort dying and not living.'

(Henning Mankell, *Ich sterbe, aber die Erinnerung lebt* [Munich, 2006], pp. 63f).

There are two contexts that have to be taken into account when inquiring into the causes of AIDS. The first, and less extensive, context is that of the epidemic spread of AIDS and the causes of new infections. The other context has to do with the history of Africa and Europe, which is an ever-present background to the origin of the AIDS pandemic and concerns the ethics of globalization. In the case of the first context, reference to the history of colonialization and the social divisions of recent decades misses the point.

The second context, however, is the correct location for such an inquiry. Mankell's concern has to be tackled in two steps.

A short survey should throw some light on the actual causes of HIV/AIDS. In 2005 there were about four million new AIDS infections, and about 2.8 million died of the disease. In the early decades individual risk factors were usually at the forefront of discussion and of preventative programmes. Now, however, the emphasis is increasingly on structural and social factors that favour new infections and the spread of the disease. They are closely interwoven with the individual factors, and therefore much more stress is laid on them in preventative programmes.

Accordingly, drug addicts, for example, are singled out for a share of the responsibility because of the multiple use of hypodermic needles – and a third of new infections across the world are ascribable to injected drug abuse, but only if southern Africa is left out of account. East European and Asian countries in particular have vast problems because of rising drug abuse in recent years, which is favoured, for instance, by the increasing popularity of opium poppy cultivation in Afghanistan and by the trade in opium and heroin.[1] Yet medically controlled substitution treatments are often illegal (for instance in Russia and many East European countries) or are not applied uniformly. AIDS prevention programmes are arranged just as unsystematically.

Nevertheless, alongside these institutional causes social exclusion and discrimination are among the structurally causative factors of the still high new infection rates and of the spread of AIDS. Exclusion, stigmatization, and social as well as institutional discrimination are also observably directed against gay men. Homosexuality is against the law in more than 50 per cent of African countries. For a long time now, studies on AIDS prevention have not taken the behaviour of gay men into account – although this ought to be a *sine qua non* of pinpointed prevention programmes.[2] In Asian countries such as Thailand or Cambodia, moreover, sex between men is not included as a risk factor in national epidemiological AIDS studies, although the new infection rate is dramatically high precisely among male homosexuals.

Nevertheless, the question of how Africa is affected is especially urgent. One third of all people infected with HIV worldwide live in countries south of the Sahara, as do about one half of all women in the world who are infected or directly threatened with infection.[3] By now it is possible to identify the individual causes of the high infection rate. In addition to homosexual sex and drug use with needles we can cite *herpes simplex* infections, uncircumcised men, not using condoms, first sexual intercourse at a young age, and – obviously – unprotected sex among married couples.

Restricting sex to married intercourse has proved not to be an automatic defence against AIDS, but in certain circumstances is held to promise a security that is actually very far from guaranteed – a fact that ought to be stated more emphatically by church workers in the field in Africa.[4] But the high rate of mobility in southern Africa is also one of the reasons for the spread of AIDS. Causes that seem to be individual in nature almost always point to the more deeply entrenched structural problems. This is evident in the inadequate availability of preventative means. The Global HIV Prevention Working Group says that currently three condoms could be distributed per man per year in sub-Saharan countries, which means a dearth of almost two billion condoms a year.[5] In this respect, individual causes – lack of care in sexual activity, say– and structural causes – inadequate information and education and inadequate access to protective resources – go increasingly hand in hand. But we also have to take into account other structural causes that cannot be opposed solely by combating HIV/AIDS, but only by overlapping social and cultural changes. They include stopping infringements of women's rights such as gender-specific discrimination against women by forced sex, enforced unprotected sex, and/or sexual violence inside and outside marriage, but also an unequal distribution of educational opportunities and a neglectful attitude to establishing pinpointed prevention programmes. To combat the causes and the spread of the disease effectively, we must have, first, appropriately targeted prevention (and the associated research); second, vaccination programmes (and research); third, research into and development of forms of treatment that are also suitable for the resistant forms of the virus; and, fourth, distribution systems that actually reach those affected.[6]

The other context with regard to causes concerns the continent of Africa in relation to globalization. The globalized world is a disordered, unjustly networked world. This disorder has its own history.

In the first phase of globalization – since the end of the seventeenth century – those areas which Europeans saw as 'new', 'uncivilized', or 'uninhabited' were established as dependent territories. The people, cultures, and traditions of these areas either remained invisible or were made invisible by resolute repression. In a second – chronologically indeterminate – phase of globalization the dependent countries gained a new self-awareness and campaigned or fought for an independence they achieved to varying degrees. The third phase of globalization, which we are now experiencing, is characterized by *new markets* (internationally connected currency and capital markets), *new tools* (internet connections, mobile phones, media networks), and *new actors* (a World Trade Organization with directional competence in regard to national governments, transnational groups with an economic power greater than that of many States, and networks of non-governmental organizations whose activities extend over and beyond national frontiers). Another novel feature is the *compression of space and time*, so that time accelerates and space shrinks. In terms of the speed at which we move in the world – in, that is, the real and not the virtual, world – this world has become fifty times smaller since Columbus.

For many countries with a history of violent subjugation, this means the establishment of new, not fewer, violent forms of dependence. Within these processes of dependency, independence, and new dependence a belief has emerged that 'the West' has manufactured the AIDS virus for Africa. This is an attempt to interpret suffering and the inexplicable so that the explanation apparently both accords with one's own historical experience and affords one some degree of dignity.

Any such attempt to affirm dignity is questionable and frail. It divides humankind into pure victims and sheer victimizers and is quite contrary to what is urgently needed and what the countries of the northern hemisphere should make their first priority: the initiation of a new phase of globalization, in which conflicts between dependence and independence are exchanged for a firm political and cultural consciousness of interdependence. A feeling of interdependence based on the experience of the vulnerability of our common humanity, and leading to the institution of structures of justice, will endow this divided and fragile humankind with the space it needs in which to develop.

3.

Back to Christine. The medicines that she used cost exactly twice as much as she earned each month as a teacher. She took home about four hundred kronor a month. The drugs, in the least expensive form available, cost eight hundred kronor. . . . History books of the future will dedicate a chapter to the activities of the big pharmaceutical monopolies and their shareholders and directors when the AIDS epidemic was raging across the world. But there will be no courts in which to arraign the dead entrepreneurs who were responsible.

(Henning Mankell, *Ich sterbe, aber die Erinnerung lebt* [Munich, 2006], p. 70).

In bioethics, Christine's problem, which Henning Mankell describes exactly, is one of 'equal access' to health resources or drugs. Something that seems so simple from an abstract ethical viewpoint becomes complicated as soon as the theory of justice is fully focussed on the economic aspects. Pharmaceutical research, development, and production in particular are subject to general (global) market conditions: that is, competition between suppliers who have invested previously in research into and development of medicines and therefore acquire patent production of their intellectual property right in return for disclosing information. The implementation of the principle of equal treatment in the same circumstances, on which the principle of justice is based,[7] requires competition to be controlled, but without endangering it within the globalized economic system. It is not a lack of *knowledge*, but a lack of *governance* that is the problem in the injustice of the struggle against disease, not only of HIV/AIDS. Accordingly, the WHO report of 2005 states with regard to the groups of mothers, newborn babies, and children who dramatically lack health care (and represent a constantly growing problematical group): 'There is no doubt that the technical knowledge exists to respond to many, if not most, of the critical health problems and hazards that affect the health and survival of mothers, newborns, and children.'

It has been shown that, given minimal regulation of health research in recent decades, only about 1 per cent of research funds is devoted to infectious diseases, even though they comprise about 12 per cent of all illnesses and research has been largely supported by public funds. There is controversy about the possibility of establishing equilibrium between the right to 'essential drugs', the right to freedom of research, and the preservation of intellectual property right.[8] It is an urgent question how theories of justice and political theories might respond to Mankell's justifiable indignation about the injustice of access to medicines. A central concern is that the principle of equality makes it necessary to impose a corrective unequal treatment, for example by means of the already implemented differential price systems for medicines.

A major instance might serve to show how the conflict between different rights affects the treatment of AIDS, since insufficient – or inappropriate – attention is paid to the *connection* between rights of freedom and social rights and to the *weighting* of human rights.

In accordance with the so-called TRIPS agreement (the convention on Trade-Related Intellectual Property Rights) of 1994, the intellectual property rights for the WTO States were reformed in favour of the pharmaceutical companies, who were intent on making sure that development costs were compensated for by patents. In 2001 a supplementary statement was approved in the form of the so-called Doha declaration on public health, which had far-reaching consequences for AIDS research and care.[9] Accordingly, the issue of compulsory licences is allowed in urgent situations. This was confirmed in 2003, and thus the way was opened up for a better, that is, a less expensive form of care with medical drugs. On the one hand, the WTO States had to implement the patent directives, and thus in principle place innovations under patent protection. But, on the other hand, this agreement also accommodates the unequal treatment principle, which forms part of the theory of justice and requires corrective and compensatory measures to be taken in the case of an unjust *status quo*. This is included in the TRIPS agreement to the extent that compulsory licenses are permitted which, first, allow the *production* of generics for one's own use, and, second, favour the *export* of generics in underdeveloped countries (cf. the example of Brazil as considered in this issue of *Concilium*).

These provisions were not understood and therefore communicated as a necessary part of a policy based on justice and harmonization but were devised as concessions to the developing countries or to the non-governmental organizations working on their behalf. Accordingly, they were seen more as a form of political compromise than as an ethically requisite directive decision to be implemented politically. Furthermore, in practice pressure was exerted on countries to introduce compulsory licenses – recourse to compulsory licenses counts as an exceptional arrangement, although an inadequate supply of health-care products is normal in those regions most affected by AIDS. The World Trade Organization requires the agreement with member States to be implemented as far as possible in accordance with comprehensive patent protection, which means, for instance, that the transitional time limit for compulsory licenses expired on 1 January 2005.

India is one of the countries with a patent law since 1 January 2005 that accords with the TRIPS and Doha agreement. This is wholly in the interest of the State because India has an aspiring pharmaceutical industry and in the meantime has the biggest share of exported generics. Therefore the NGO *Médecins sans frontières* has the following to say of the supply of AIDS drugs and India: 'Indian generics are the mainstay of our HIV/AIDS programme in thirty countries. Eighty per cent of the more than 80,000 patients whom we treat receive 80 per cent of Indian generic products.'

Therefore there will be no problem about supplying developing countries in particular with AIDS generics as long as India receives compulsory licenses. But the TRIPS agreement provided for a temporary period that closed on 1 January 2005. Since then India has had to guarantee patent protection. Here the problems start that were only apparently resolved by the supplementary declaration of 2003.

In the course of the last year a legal dispute blew up as a result of the Indian Patent Office refusing a patent to the Swiss pharmaceutical company Novartis because the product in question exhibited only slight differences from the original drug.[10] Thereupon Novartis entered an appeal to maintain the validity of the patent. But patent protection could put the life-saving drug even more out of the reach of patients like Christine:

> While fierce generic competition has helped prices for first-line AIDS drug regimen to fall by 99% from $10,000 to roughly $130 per patient per year since 2000, prices for second-line drugs – which patients need as resistance develops naturally – remain high due to increased patent barriers in key generics-producing countries like India. In a country such as South Africa, where MSF has been providing antiretroviral therapy for five years, treating 58 patients on second-line drugs costs the same as treating over 550 patients on first-line. In addition, newer HIV medicines that are recommended by WHO can cost up to 50 times more, if they are even available in countries. These drugs will be impossible to use unless generic competition drives down prices and helps increase availability.[11]

The Novartis argument takes quite the opposite direction with regard to access to medical drugs: it is assured precisely *by means of* the patent, and almost all Indian patients obtained free access to cancer therapy with Glivec through the patient-aid programme financed by Novartis.

Irrespective of the outcome of this legal dispute, this example shows that the people who are most urgently in need of medicines easily become the playthings of the economic interests of those on whom they truly depend for their lives. If the big companies are motivated by incentives received at all stages: from research and development, from patent protection, and finally from production conditions, they will show a marketing-oriented interest in the justifiable claims of people to treatment available on principle. If the incentive systems do not work, then obviously rights won't count. As so often happens, in the above case Novartis responded with a *generous gesture* (aid programmes for patients), instead of acknowledging the patients' *rights* to care. In ethical terminology, justice is pitted against love, which replaces a duty of justice with a (non-enforceable) duty of virtue.

Mankell's indignation is directed last, but not least, against this aspect of the AIDS pandemic – because economic interests *should not be pitted* against patients' rights. But his aim goes awry when he critically cites the 'shareholders' and 'company directors' who will not have to stand trial and thereby personalizes the problem. A personalization of this kind is not very helpful, because what we are concerned with is a structural problem of economic policy. Instead what we need is public research and development that is aimed at discovering appropriate preventative measures and medicines and is guided by ethical considerations, as well as a form of social accompaniment and care: that is, measures to spur the economy *with conditions and requirements that obey the principle of justice*. It is indeed scandalous that to date all this has not been implemented for political reasons, so that there is no threat to the competitive situation. *This* is a scandal which theologians and the Church ought to expatiate on for good reasons and with reference to their own tradition of social teaching (see L. Cahill's article in this issue).[12]

You cannot base effective politico-ethical or socio-ethical discussion and judgments on anthropological principles with a narrow moral-theological bias, which are tied to a sexual ethos relying on married couples' acceptance of readiness to conceive as the basic principle of their sexual morality, and whose main function is seen as criticism of the ways in which those affected live their lives. The studies, debates, and assessments we need are those more concerned with solving problems than with maintaining an abstract moral order. Theologians are called on to respond to structural injustice – in the form of a theologically-motivated and philosophically-grounded theory of justice to be implemented politically. The Church must exert itself to establish and promote respect for the right of all human beings to the treatment of their illness, in so far as preventative measures, vaccines, and forms of treatment are available in principle. This right is not restricted merely to *actual* availability since a lack of financial possibilities cannot be adduced seriously, or at least not as an ethical argument for the non-existent programme. Otherwise human rights would be subordinated to economic conditions (and to the interests of the actors of a specific sector of the economy).

In the medium term, the 'option for justice' means, first, conditional research that has to be oriented to the investigation of neglected diseases and essential drugs; and, second, an overhaul of the patent system along the lines of the WHO report, which says that extensive adjustments are required. In the short term, however, it means the introduction and, if necessary, even the extension of the possibility of compulsory state licences for producing

generics, and, third, structural aid facilities in the sense of the millennium
target, in order to make it possible to fight poverty effectively as a factor in
the origin of disease and its non-treatment.

4.

She had begun to join her illness and she watched her sister and brother
from a distance, as if she were on a train and they stood on a platform
watching it pull away. And, as if she were on a train, she felt sadness
mingled with relief, a surprising and perverse contentment at the sheer
fact of going somewhere while others stayed behind. . . . She could join
the illness and not worry anymore. . . . When Zoe saw Jamal she left and
came back into the room because she felt no pleasure, not even a secret
hint of it, in leaving her son. He hung back. He looked at her with an angry
glint of non-recognition. She tried to stay in the room for him. She tried
to smell like herself. Was she smiling? She lifted her hand . . . and held it
out to Jamal. He stepped back and for the first time Zoe heard a voice that
was not a voice, that did not speak in words but rolled through her like a
stone. Give him his terror and his hatred and whatever he chooses to
remember of love and let him be.

(Michael Cunningham, *Flesh and Blood* (New York, 1995), pp. 416f).

The main thing about dying of AIDS is, of course, that you die. But it is
often more than that. It often means dying prematurely. It is not dying when
life has been lived to an appropriate age, but a form of dying in which those
who die cannot simply surrender themselves to death, because they – as
mothers for instance – know that they have to leave behind them far too
many things that still have to be dealt with, and far too many people.

Furthermore it is often a form of dying with a stigma: dying beset with
guilt. This is not merely the existential guilt of a human life, and not only the
subjective experience of the guilt of deserting other people. It is a matter of
the social stigmatizing of an 'immoral' disease for which, in others' eyes
(whether they know this or imagine it), 'you yourself are responsible.'

A stop must be put to both aspects of AIDS.

Dying prematurely from a disease for which – in principle – medicines
exist is bound up with injustice and unequal treatment – a scandal that
people have to be made aware of and has to be brought to an end.

The stigmatizing of the disease and the stigmatizing of suffering human
beings constitute a similar scandal.

To bring about the decisive changes that are needed we must have not only political structures, economic justice, research funds, and much else, but also histories, stories, narratives.

We are all 'involved in histories of one kind or another' (Schapp). These narratives are the text and context of a life, and events become experiences in the hermeneutical process of understanding history in terms of these life-histories.

In them the people become visible who otherwise are often concealed behind statistics, structures, and experimental results.

In the great drama known as 'HIV/AIDS' that is unfolding on the world stage, life-histories offer us the possibility of, as it were, an infectious reaction.

We must willingly succumb to this particular form of infection not in order to let the disease have the last word, the ultimate judgment, and final victory, but in order to respond to the stories of our fellow-humans, in order to acknowledge their fellow-humanity and, finally, to act on that recognition.

6.

Of course the truth about AIDS is a general truth regarding the present condition of the world. In other words: the way in which we allow it to exist.
(Henning Mankell, *Ich sterbe, aber die Erinnerung lebt* [Munich, 2006], p. 80).

Translated by J. G. Cumming

Notes

1. United Nations Office on Drugs and Crime (Unodc), *World Drug Report for 2005*, Geneva, 2006.
2. Unaids, *2006 Report on the Global Aids Epidemic*, Geneva, 2006.
3. *Ibid.*
4. Chris Beyrer, 'IV Epidemiology Update and Transmission Factors: Risks and Risk Contexts – 16th International Aids Conference Epidemiology Plenary', in: *Clinical Infectious Diseases* 44 (2007), 981–7.
5. Global HIV Prevention Working Group, *HIV Prevention in the Era of Expanded Treatment Access*, San Francisco, 2006.
6. *World Health Report 2004*, Geneva, 2005.

7. See the critique of this presumption of equality in A. Krebs (ed.), *Gleichheit oder Gerechtigkeit. Texte der neuen Egalitarismuskritik*, Frankfurt a. M., 2000.

8. Cf. in this regard the WHO report on intellectual property, which clearly outlines the inadequacies of health care also with regard to the patent system: http://www.who.int/intellectualproperty/report/en/index.html.

9. See, e.g., for a detailed discussion: Frederick M. Abbott, 'The WTO Medicines decision: World Pharmaceutical Trade and the Protection of Public Health', in *The American Journal of International Law* 99, No. 317 (2005), 317–58.

10. The drug in question is Glivec, which is used to treat leukaemia. The case is also thought of as a kind of exemplary action, since it will also influence the patentability of AIDS drugs. On the *Médecins sans frontières* campaign see: http://www.aerzte-ohne-grenzen.de/Presse/Pressemitteilungen/2007/Pressemitteilung-2007-03-05.php (last accessed on 14 Mar. 2007). For legal references see: http://www.lawyerscollective.org/ (last accessed on 14 Mar. 2007).

11. Médecins sans frontières: http://www.accessmed-msf.org/prod/publications.asp?scntid=1411200692472&contenttype=PARA&, 14.11.2007 (accessed 12 Mar. 2007)

12. In this respect, to be sure, we must not ignore the fact that for a long time the Church also avoided any criticism of economic structures. In the nineteenth century the property question was a main element of defence against Communism, and, in the compendium of social doctrine, health care is very, very low down the list of concerns. Instead, this work conceives of social ethics so overwhelmingly from the viewpoint of moral theology that its real nature as an aspect of social theory all but disappears.

DOCUMENTATION

Jon Sobrino – Dossier

A Message from the Presidium of the European Society for Catholic Theology regarding the Notification on the works of Jon Sobrino

It is with sadness and sorrow that the Presidium of the European Society for Catholic Theology has received the *Notification* on the works of our Salvadorian colleague, Jon Sobrino. The Society wonders whether its publication was either necessary or desirable, for it appears that it does not only do harm to a theologian of international academic renown but also to the discipline of theology itself.

At first sight, the text of the Notification seems to be written very prudently and clearly avoids any condemnation of the person. A closer reading, however, reveals some problematic aspects, of which the disregard of the theological developments of the last fifty years would seem to be the most serious and disturbing one. Irrespective of the results of recent exegetical, historical-theological, and systematic-theological research, the text develops a foremost deductive argument which suffers from a remarkable lack of hermeneutical-theological consciousness. For example, quotations from Scripture, Conciliar documents, and recent Papal statements are indiscriminately put together with theological concepts and arguments from a diverse provenance. (. . .)

The European Society for Catholic Theology fears that with this Notification not only is the theological work of one of the leading Catholic theologians discredited, but also, and once again, the cause of liberation theology as well, which precisely because of its ongoing critical-productive force remains significant for the Church at large.

Faculty of Catholic Theology, University of Münster

The members of the Faculty of Catholic Theology of the University of Münster wish to record their deep concern at the notification of censure of the Salvadoran liberation theologian Jon Sobrino by the Congregation for Doctrine. In 1998 the University awarded Sobrino an honorary doctorate for his theological work, his efforts to promote a Church whose life includes a decisive option for the poor, and his personal witness. This award expressed our high estimate of Jon Sobrino's theological work and of his witness of faith which the Faculty sees no reason to revise in any respect. All those interested are expressly referred to Professor Giancarlo Collet's address of commendation of Jon Sobrino. He emphatically praised Sobrino's exemplary combination of scholarly achievement and courageous commitment to the cause of justice and peace. (. . .)

The *Notification* itself does not express any such sanctions, but relegates any decision about them entirely to the competent church authorities. It is to be hoped that these bodies will prefer further untrammelled theological discussion to measures that will cause more distress to the faithful than could result from a few trenchant expressions. After all, a theology that acknowledges its commitment to Jesus' proclamation of the kingdom of God has to take sides. Surely solidarity with the poor and oppressed people of Latin America and the whole world is its only possible application? The Faculty of Catholic Theology of this University is prepared to offer more detailed comments on the Sobrino memorandum if this proves necessary.

From the Directorate of the Society for Theology and Religious Studies, SOTER–BRAZIL

We express our solidarity with Sobrino at this time of perplexity and pain. His Christological writings have been appreciated not only for the love they show for the poor of our continent of Latin America and the Caribbean but also for their recognized and exemplary achievement in following a method-ological path that makes the Good News of Jesus Christ meaningful for our present situation. Sobrino seeks to show us how starting from a reading of the full humanity of Jesus of Nazareth opens the way to a deeper apprecia-tion of the divine dimension of his innermost being, which comes from the Father. The Son of God followed this way in obscurity, in humility, in self-bestowal, and in death in solidarity with the suffering of the world, which is revealed in the suffering of the poor.

We regret that an understanding of Jesus Christ 'from above', top-down, as shown in the *Notification* places it in opposition to the thrust of current theological endeavour, especially that of Latin American liberation theo-logy, which follows the way 'from below', bottom-up, and in this way recovers the historical face of Jesus and his practice that led him to the cross, so as to recognize in him the one the Father sent as Preacher of the Kingdom and great sacrament of his love for us. (. . .)

From the Central American University of El Salvador (UCA)

We have received the *Notification*, as has Fr Sobrino, and have done so with serenity and respect. (. . .) At this point it is appropriate to list six positive points we have drawn from this experience:

- It is not a matter of silencing anyone (. . .);
- There is no condemnation of liberation theology (. . .);
- There is no condemnation of Jon Sobrino's theology (. . .);
- There is no implication for Archbishop Romero's theology (. . .);
- There is no implication for the preferential option for the poor (. . .);
- The experience has strengthened our solidarity.

On the day following the publicaton of the *Notification* on Jon Sobrino several representatives of different lay communities arrived to express their solidarity with Fr Sobrino at this difficult time he was going through. His Jesuit brethren also surrounded their venerated theologian and consoled him with a welcoming hug. (. . .)

Declaration by the John XXIII Association of Theologians on the *Notification* from the Congregation for the Doctrine of the Faith concerning Jon Sobrino

1. We believe Sobrino's reflection on Jesus of Nazareth to be one of the most important and influential in twentieth-century Christian theology, one that has enlightened the faith of believers and inspired their commitment to solidarity with the poor and excluded, while contributing to giving meaning and relevance to the figure of Jesus.

2. One of the main contributions made by Sobrino's Christology is to have recovered the humanity and historical character of Jesus of Nazareth, while at the same time emphasizing his divine condition, within the best Christian tradition running from the New Testament to the present, as is recognized by the highly qualified theologians who have minutely analyzed the work of the Spanish–Salvadoran theologian.

(. . .)

5. The Vatican *Notification* forgets theological principles officially adopted by the papal magisterium, such as 'the Church of the poor', which was the principle that inspired John XXIII to convoke the Second Vatican Council: 'The Church', he said, 'presents herself to unerdeveloped nations as she is and seeks to be, as Church: as *Church of all and, particularly, Church of the poor*.'

(. . .)

8. We see the absence of sanctions from the *Notification* as a positive sign. Should these be issued subsequently, however, we should view them as unjust and contrary to the gospel.

The case of Jon Sobrino and the present situation of theology – Professor Peter Hünermann

(. . .) The foregoing summary of the objections and the account of the pronouncements and approaches favoured by Jon Sobrino should have made it clear to theologically aware readers that not only Jon Sobrino but the most respected exegetes and systematic theologians – Catholic and Protestant – stand together in the ranks of those accused. Indeed, in his writings – this could not be expressed adequately in the foregoing – Jon Sobrino conducts an intensive dialogue with his Protestant and Catholic colleagues in systematic theology.

In contradistinction to his projected Christology, the *Notification* proposes one in which the pronouncements of conciliar theology are said to be already discernible as the same propositions in the texts of the New Testament. The arguments of the memorandum are carried on wholly in terms of the 'metaphysical' conceptual models also used by the councils. The decisive notions are the divine and the human nature of Jesus Christ, the hypostatic union, the doctrine of the anhypostatic status of the human nature of Jesus Christ, and the scholastic version of Aristotelian causal theory. All this amounts to proposing a condensed version of neo-scholastic Christology as the criterion of contemporary theology. Hence the astonishment which the memorandum has aroused among theologians. It is impossible to reconcile updated exegetical findings or more modern systematic theological propositions with this neo-scholastic model. With serious misgivings, we have to ask if this kind of theology – an eye of the needle indeed – is to be the only 'gateway' through which theological work and research have to pass in the future? Finally, does this *Notification* represent the first major public act of the new Prefect of the Congregation for the

Doctrine of the Faith and his team of helpers? More than that, could this also be the new model for Benedict XVI's policy regarding theology? (. . .)

What is the sum total of the foregoing? Two conclusions predominate:

1. Inevitably, the relationship between the Pope and bishops on the one hand, and theologians on the other hand, is extremely important with regard to the course to be followed by the Church in the future. At present the Congregation for the Doctrine of the Faith assumes the prime function in the 'quality control' of theology. It sees its task as ensuring that theology is an authentic exposition of the *ratio fidei*. In this respect, serious conflicts have constantly arisen since the second half of the nineteenth century that have damaged the reputation of the Church and its development in faith. The responsibility for these conflicts is not attributable merely to the individuals working in the Congregation and to their comprehensive or, as the case may be, scarcely profound education and training. Inadequacies of this kind are liable to spark conflicts. The essential reason for this situation is that Congregation for the Doctrine of the Faith – the successor to the Holy Office – retains the fundamental structure of the kind of board of censors of the early modern era maintained by all European States at one time. The nature of modern quality-control facilities in the area of the sciences and scholarly research projects is quite different. Essentially, these instances work in conjunction with the sciences and – as far as possible – the authoritative scientific bodies are included in decision processes affecting policy and administration in the field of sciences and scholarship. In the present-day world, the *ratio fidei* has to be developed in a highly-complex advanced civil society with its own specific and serious social, economic and human problems and dislocations. Consequently, the organization and methodology of a censorship authority of another age are totally inappropriate to the degree of complexity proper to a society of this kind. The Congregation for the Doctrine of the Faith is desperately in need of what is known nowadays as an intelligent makeover.

2. With regard to the specific case under consideration here, the condemnation of Jon Sobrino's writings, it is not only appropriate but necessary to follow up the present *Notification* – as with the statements about liberation theology – with a second *Notification* of a different inclination.

Our Solidarity with theologian Jon Sobrino

We the undersigned, theologians, biblicists, social scientists, community assessors, and pastors of Christian Churches in Brazil, witness our solidarity with Jon Sobrino, a theologian living in El Salvador, inserted in the conflict-ridden reality of Central America. Sobrino is the author of major works that have nourished our faith in Jesus Christ and in the Kingdom of God. At the time when the Vatican is censuring his theology, we publicly express our confidence in the evangelical character of his life and his works; our sadness at the shadows of fundamentalism; our hope that respect and the spirit of dialogue may prevail.

ANTÔNIO CECCHIN, BENEDITO FERRARO, CLÁUDIO DE OLIVEIRA RIBEIRO, EDSON FERNANDO DE ALMEIDA, FREI BETTO, FAUSTINO COUTO TEIXEIRA, FERNANDO ALTEMEYER JÚNIOR, FRANCISCO OROFINO, JETHER PEREIRA RAMALHO, JOÃO BATISTA LIBÂNIO, JOSÉ OSCAR BEOZZO, JÚLIO DE SANTA ANA, LEONARDO BOFF, LÚCIA RIBEIRO, LUCÍLIA G. PEREIRA RAMALHO, LUIZ ALBERTO G. DE SOUZA, LUIZ EDUARDO WANDERLEY, MAGALI DO N. CUNHA, MANFREDO ARAÚJO DE OLIVEIRA, MARCELO BARROS, MARCIA MIRANDA, MARIA HELENA ARROCHELLAS, MARIA TEREZA BUSTAMANTE TEIXEIRA, MARIA TEREZA SARTÓRIO, PATRÍCIA COUTINHO, PEDRO A. R. DE OLIVEIRA, SÉRGIO COUTINHO, VIOLAINE DE SANTA ANA, WALDEMAR ROSSI, MARIA BEATRIZ SIMÕES DA PAIXAO, ROSELI CONSOLI DO PRADO, BERNADETE GASPAR

From Claude Geffré, O.P.

I have always admired Jon Sobrino for his reinterpretation of Christology on the basis of the innocent suffering of the poor of Latin America. Twenty years ago I was happy and proud to publish his book *Jesus in Latin America* in the series 'Cogitatio Fidei'. It still has world-wide relevance. This belated *Notification* by the Congregation for the Doctrine of the Faith regarding Jon Sobrino's original work is altogether inopportune now that since the fall of the Berlin Wall Marxist ideology is no longer a temptation to Christian theologians. The very serious crisis of credibility affecting the Church today has many other causes. Rather than facing up to the growing split within the Catholic Church across the world, it seems that the Vatican's sole concerns are to settle its scores with liberation theologians and to resolve the *schism* provoked by some thousands of behind-the-times followers of Archbishop Lefebvre. (. . .)

From 'Cristianisme i Justícia'

We should like to share some first thoughts with our friends, since Jon Sobrino has always worked closely with our 'Cristianisme i Justícia' Study Centre, and because a dozen of its members have been or are regular lecturers at the 'Archbishop Romero Centre' at the Central American University of El Salvador, directed by Jon Sobrino.

1. A document from the Congregation for the Doctrine of the Faith does not mean the complete banning of an author. (. . .)

2. This is not the moment to engage with the whole content of this lengthy Roman document. (. . .)

3. In circumstances that many might find a source of suffering and even of scandal, we are moved to make these observations by the mandate from the biblical prophet: '"Comfort my people", says the Lord'. (. . .)

4. We are grateful that the *Notification*, in its present form, contains, apart from detailed comments, no sanction or prohibition on Jon Sobrino's writing. (. . .)

5. Today we should feel we are Church. (. . .)

A document such as this is a fact that we Christians have to accept as a painful reality that forms part of our life in the Church. As one simple aid, among others, to this reflection, we recommend reading Victor Codina's Notebook in our series 'Ayudar': 'Feeling Church in the Church's Winter'.

Comment of the Faculty of Catholic Theology of the University of Vienna on the *Notification* regarding the work of Jon Sobrino, SJ, issued by the Vatican Congregation for the Doctrine of the Faith

The Faculty of Catholic theology of the University of Vienna is astonished to learn of the condemnation of Jon Sobrino's major works on Christology. The Faculty has come to appreciate Jon Sobrino as a theologian whose life and thought are entirely marked by the experience of Christ's presence in the poor. Even the memorandum of the Congregation for the Doctrine of the Faith commends Sobrino's 'concern for the poor and for the oppressed' as well as the subjective intentions of his theological work. This makes it all the more surprising that such weighty objections against the theological work of one of the most outstanding theologians of the day should be raised in so summary a process. Under the present Pope there have been repeated emphatic references to the special relationship of the Christian faith to the

European Enlightenment. But any such acknowledgement of reason must be demonstrated – as is characteristic of the undeniable European inheritance – in the form of debate and dialogue in the course of which all participants submit to criticism. Accordingly, the very credibility of the Church's commitment to reason is at stake in its dealings with theology. In this sense, the Faculty of Catholic theology of this University emphatically requests the Congregation for the Doctrine of the Faith, and those church authorities concerned with the Sobrino case, to desist from disciplinary measures and to conduct the confrontation both with Sobrino's theology and with liberation theology in general, with Sobrino as one of its main representatives, in the context of serious and patient dialogue. This requires not only respect for Sobrino as a person whose witness to faith is indisputable but respect for the achievements of the theological scholarship of recent decades evident in Sobrino's work.

Manifesto by participants in the Second World Forum on Theology and Liberation

Jon Sobrino, who changed his position in society after encountering the poor people and their suffering in El Salvador, is our theological grand-master.

His written work, especially his Christology, is born of gospel experience, of his 'epistemological rupture' and his discovery of the 'theological place' that is the poor. And the poor are by far the majority of the People that is Church. (. . .) In rigorous Christological terms, Sobrino is the master who is assisting more than one generation to make the leap from abstract dogma, from the dogmatic dream, to the encounter with the Christ alive in his context, in his theological place: that is, the poor. (. . .)

We are convinced that if this Christology of Sobrino causes any disquiet, this has less to do with dogmatic doctrine than with practical attitudes. (. . .) The disquiet may give rise to rupture with that dogmatic formalism which serves ecclesiastical formalism. It may give rise to conversion to this theological place of revelation, of the Reign of God, of salvation. (. . .)

[full text on wftl.org, under News and Events]

Lay People of El Salvador express solidarity with Jon Sobrino

We are grateful for the contribution made by Fr Jon's theological reflection, we recognize his identification with the witness of the martyrs, and we stand by him at this difficult time. . . . We rejoice that there is no admonition, as this would have been an injustice against someone we recognize as a theologian of mercy and justice, but we are worried that the *Notification* should be made public without taking the impact it might cause into account.

From the Executive Committee of the Community for Ecumenical Education in Latin America and the Caribbean (CETELA)

In a certain way, Sobrino has now become, involuntarily, the symbol of a message from the Vatican to those who still keep good memories of Vatican II (1962–5) and of the meetings of bishops at Medellín (1968) and Puebla (1979). (. . .) If the Christian Church spiritualizes the gospel of the Crucified, who identifies himself with the crucified of our time in this fashion, we have to ask if it has understood what Matthew says in his Gospel, repeating Jesus' words: 'I was hungry and you gave me food, I was thirsty and you gave me something to drink, I was a stranger and you welcomed me, I was naked and you gave me clothing, I was sick and you took care of me, I was in prison and you visited me' (Matt. 25.35ff). For Sobrino, mercy is at the origin of the divine and the human.

Religious Reflection Team (ERT) of the Conference of Religious of Brazil (CRB), on the CDF *Notification* regarding the Christology of Jon Sobrino

The Religious Reflection Team of the Conference of Religious of Brazil feels called to declare itself, in a spirit of ecclesial sharing, following the CDF's *Notification* regarding Jon Sobrino's Christology. As a Jesuit religious and a theologian with a living commitment to the course of religious life in Latin America, Jon Sobrino has helped us substantially through his theological and, specifically, Christological meditations and studies. Suffice to recall his enlightening reflection on the presence of religious life, 'in the desert, on the periphery and the frontier', in the line of the missionary 'vanguard' recognized in *Evangelii Nuntiandi*.

We have studied Jon Sobrino's Christology since its beginnings, and it has strengthened the reality of the mystery of God present in Jesus and in the experience of following him through immersing ourselves in solidarity with human circumstances. He taught us to be realistic in recognizing the face of God in the human face of the Son of God, without having problems with Christological dogma. (. . .) This makes us surprised at the CDF's use of terms such as 'harm', 'errors and dangers', and 'discrepancy with the faith of the Church' in relation to Jon Sobrino's writings. His writings have, on the contrary, encouraged our faith in Jesus, true God and true Man, as well as our reconciling this faith with the victimizing and anti-evangelical reality we face. In a way, the note of 'urgency' struck by the *Notification* leads us to imagine that a negative judgment was made at the outset and that it is an attempt to influence the direction taken by the forthcoming Fifth General Conference of Latin American Bishops, while at the same time reminding us of other authoritarian strategies adopted in our history.

We should like to understand the *Notification*, which we feel applies to us too, as an invitation to open and participatory debate. (. . .)

'The truth, Pilate, is . . .' – Pedro Casaldáliga

(. . .) I wrote to Jon Sobrino, reminding him that we who keep company with him are millions, and that, above all, Jesus of Nazareth keeps company with him. (. . .) 'Through your blessed fault', I told Jon, 'many of us are hearing, shot through with relevance, Jesus' decisive question: "And you, who do you say that I am?" Because it is the true Jesus that we want to follow.'

With domineering disdain Pilate asks Jesus what truth is, but he does not wait for an answer, hands him over to be killed, and washes his hands. Maxence van der Meersch answers Pilate and answers for us all: 'The truth, Pilate, is being on the side of the poor.' Religion and politics have to accept this answer with all its ultimate implications. The whole of Jesus' life, furthermore, is this same answer. The option for the poor defines the whole of politics and the whole of religion. Once it was, 'Outside the Church there is no salvation'; then it was, 'Outside the world there is no salvation'. Jon Sobrino reminds us, once again, that, 'Outside the poor there is no salvation'. John XXIII pleaded for 'a Church of the poor, so that it may become the Church of all'. The fact is that the poor, with their denied lives and death 'before their time', define the truth or the falsity of any society, any Church. Our Jon Sobrino tells us: 'Those who have not explicitly known God have already met God if they loved the poor'; and the gospel repeatedly says the same in Jesus' words and life, in his manger and on his cross, in the Beatitudes, in the parables, in the Last Judgment. (. . .)

Contributors

The Editors

REGINA AMMICHT QUINN is Professor of Ethics at the Interdepartmental Centre for Ethics in the Sciences and Humanities at the University of Tübingen. Her fields of interests are questions of fundamental and applied ethics; ethics and culture; the history of Christian devotion; gender issues. She was denied the *nihil obstat* by the Catholic Church and is not allowed to teach as a theology professor. Her recent books include *Körper, Religion und Sexualität. Theologische Reflexionen zur Ethik der Geschlechter* ([3]2004); *Glück – der Ernst des Lebens (*2006).

E-mail: regina.ammicht-quinn@uni-tuebingen.de

HILLE HAKER is Professor of Moral Theology/Social Ethics at the Catholic Faculty of Frankfurt, and a member of the European Group on Ethics in Sciences and New Technologies (EGE). From 2003 to 2005 she was Associate Professor of Christian Ethics at Harvard University, Cambridge, Mass. Her books include *Moralische Identität* (1999), *Ethik der genetischen Frühdiagnostik* (2002) and three co-edited volumes: *Ethics of Human Genome Analysis. European Perspectives* (1993), *The Ethics of Genetics in Human Procreation* (2000), and *Ethik-Geschlecht-Wissenschaften* (2006).

E-mail: Hille.haker@em.uni-frankfurt.de

The Authors:

ISABEL APAWO PHIRI is Professor of African Theology, School of Theology and Religion, at the University of KwaZulu Natal, and the General Coordinator for the Circle of Concerned African Women Theologians.

Address: Private Bag, X01, Scottsville, 3209, Pietermaritzburg, South Africa
E-mail: PhiriI@ukzn.ac.za

LISA SOWLE CAHILL has been Professor of Christian Ethics at Boston College, Mass. since 1976 and is also Visiting Professor at Georgetown and Yale Universities. Her specialities are history of Christian ethics; New Testament and ethics; Catholic social ethics; feminist theology and sex and gender ethics; bioethics; ethics of war and peace. Her recent books are *Theological Bioethics: Participation, Justice and Change* (2005); *Genetics, Theology, Ethics: An Interdisciplinary Conversation* (2005).

STEVE DOWDEN teaches German and European literature at Brandeis University. He is the author of books and essays on modern German fiction and is also the editor of various books, including *A Companion to Thomas Mann's Magic Mountain* (1999) and *German Literature, Jewish Critics* (2002).

Address: Dept. of German, Russian and Asian Languages and Literatures, MS024 Brandeis University, Waltham, Massachusetts, USA 02454-9110; Tel. 781.736.3218; fax 781.736.3207.

LISETTE EICHER, a nurse married to Peter Eicher, has five children. In 1988 she spent a year in São Paulo. Peter Eicher, who teaches at Paderborn University, accompanied his wife from time to time and organized aid in Germany and Switzerland. See www.sternderhoffnung.de for a comprehensive presentation of current work in Brazil.

   Peter Eicher is the author of several works and the editor of the *Neues Handbuch theologischer Grundbegriffe* (new full edition 2005).

E-mail: lisette.eicher@gmx.de; prof.eicher@gmx.de

JAMES F. KEENAN, S.J., is Professor of Theological Ethics at Boston College. His most recent books are *The Works of Mercy: The Heart of Catholicism* and *Church Ethics and its Organizational Context: Learning from the Sex Abuse Scandal in the Catholic Church*, edited with Jean Bartunek and Mary Ann Hinsdale.

E-mail: james.keenan.2@bc.edu

CAROL LINDSAY SMITH is a retired social worker and development worker. She set up Barnardo's Positive Options and wrote the original Memory Book. In 1996 she met Beatrice Were in Uganda and they have worked closely ever since in developing Memory Book work and related training programmes.

E-mail: cls.dev@lineone.net

BEATRICE WERE was founder and co-ordinator of NACWOLA from 1995 to 2001. She was the driving force behind establishing Memory Book workshops and developing the Memory Project training programme. Beatrice is now HIV/Aids co-ordinator for ActionAid Uganda. On 7 November 2006 she received the Human Rights Watch Defender award for her work on behalf of women living with HIV/Aids including her work on the Memory Book and Memory Project.

MAGGIE KELLY is a Social worker and freelance trainer and management consultant. Maggie was involved in all stages of producing the Memory Project training materials and coaching grassroots trainers in training and communication skills .

RORY O'BRINE is a graphic designer and website designer. He has designed and produced all the Memory Book and related training materials.

All four are now working to set up a website which will make the Memory Book and all related training materials freely available to groups or individuals who want to use them. www.memory-book.info .

GILLIAN PATERSON is an independent consultant and writer on development issues, specializing in HIV and AIDS. She worked for Christian Aid for many years, then for the Churches' Commission on Misson, and more recently, in a freelance capacity, for the World Council of Churches, the Ecumenical Advocacy Alliance, and for church- or faith-related organizations in India, the USA, Norway, and various African countries. She has written articles and books on health, on women, and on AIDS, all in the context of the global Church. She is currently completing a doctorate at Heythrop College, London, on the theological implications of AIDS-related stigma. She is a Catholic, lives in north London, and has three grandchildren.

Address: 215 Highbury Quadrant, London N5 2TE; Tel.+44 (0)20 7226 7235

ANTHONY G. REDDIE is a Research Fellow and Consultant in Black Theological Studies for the British Methodist Church and the Queen's Foundation for Ecumenical Theological Education in Birmingham. He holds a B.A. in (Church) History and a Ph.D. in Education and Practical and Contextual Theology; both degrees conferred by the University of Birmingham. He is the author of a number of books, including *Nobodies to Somebodies* (2003), *Acting in Solidarity* (2005), *Dramatizing Theologies* (2006), and *Black Theology in Transatlantic Dialogue* (2006). He is also the editor of *Black Theology: An International Journal.*

Address: The Queen's Foundation (For Ecumenical Theological Education), Somerset Road, Edgbaston, Birmingham B15 2QH, UK.
E-mail: a.g.reddie@queens.ac.uk

FRANK SANDERS was born in 1970. He studied Catholic theology and canon law in Münster and Würzburg. Since 1998 he has been Research Associate at the Institute for Canon Law of the University of Münster and has acted simultaneously as an independent lawyer in various ecclesiastical courts. He was awarded a degree in canon law in 1997 and a doctorate in Catholic theology in 2005. His dissertation was published as: *AIDS als Herausforderung für die Theologie. Eine Problematik zwischen Medizin, Moral und Recht* (Essen, 2005) (= *Münsterischer Kommentar zum Codex Iuris Canonici* 43).

Address: Institut für Kanonisches Recht, Johannisstrasse 8-10, D-48147 Münster, Germany
E-mail: sanderf@uni-muenster.de

N. M. SAMUEL graduated from the Christian Medical College in Vellore. He was trained in Immunology and Microbiology at the Middlesex Hospital Medical School in London, was awarded a Ph.D., and joined Tamilnadu Dr MGR Medical University, in Chennai, South India, in 1991. Dr Samuel is the Founder President of the AIDS Society of India. He serves as the Regional representative for Asia and the Pacific of the International AIDS Society and is the only member from India to serve on the Governing Council of this professional Society. He is a Member of the Executive Committee of the AIDS society of Asia and Pacific and serves on the scientific advisory board of Global Strategies for HIV Prevention USA.

Email: nms_mds@yahoo.com

Concilium Subscription Information

February   **2007/1**: *Pluralist Theology*

April   **2007/2**: *Land Conflicts – Land Utopias*

June   **2007/3**: *AIDS*

October   **2007/4**: *Christianity and Democracy*

December   **2007/5**: *Ages of Life and Christian Experience*

New subscribers: to receive *Concilium 2007* (five issues) anywhere in the world, please copy this form, complete it in block capitals and send it with your payment to the address below.

Please enter my subscription for *Concilium 2007*

Individuals

____ £40.00 UK
____ £60.00 overseas
____ $110.00 North America/Rest of World
____ €99.00 Europe

Institutions

____ £55.00 UK
____ £75.00 overseas
____ $140 North America/Rest of World
____ €125.00 Europe

Postage included – airmail for overseas subscribers

Payment Details:

Payment must accompany all orders and can be made by cheque or credit card

I enclose a cheque for £/$/€ _____ Payable to SCM-Canterbury Press Ltd

Please charge my Visa/MasterCard (Delete as appropriate) for £/$/€ _____

Credit card number ....

Expiry date ....

Signature of cardholder ....

Name on card ....

Telephone .... E-mail ....

Send your order to *Concilium*, SCM-Canterbury Press Ltd
13–17 Long Lane, London EC1A 9PN, UK
E-Mail: office@scm-canterburypress.co.uk

Customer service information:
All orders must be prepaid. Subscriptions are entered on an annual basis (i.e. January to December). No refunds on subscriptions will be made after the first issue of the Journal has been despatched. If you have any queries or require information about other payment methods, please contact our Customer Services department.